book *of* faith
Lenten Journey

book *of* faith
Lenten Journey

Marks of the Christian

David L. Miller

BOOK OF FAITH LENTEN JOURNEY
Marks of the Christian

For information on the Book of Faith initiative and Book of Faith resources, go to www.bookoffaith. org.

Book of Faith is an initiative of the

 Evangelical Lutheran Church in America
God's work. Our hands.

Cover design: Running Design Group
Interior design: PerfecType, Nashville, TN

This book was typeset using Dolly and Omnes.

Library of Congress Cataloging-in-Publication Data

Miller, David LeRoy.
  Book of faith Lenten journey : marks of the Christian / David L. Miller.
     p. cm.
  Includes bibliographical references.
  ISBN 978-0-8066-9764-2 (alk. paper)
  1. Lent--Prayers and devotions. 2. Bible. N.T. Romans XII, 1-15--Meditations. 3. Evangelical Lutheran Church in America--Prayers and devotions. I. Title.
  BV85.M54 2009
  242'.34--dc22
                              2009040914

The paper used in this publication meets the minimum requirements of American National Standard for Information Sciences—Permanence of Paper for Printed Library Materials, ANSI Z329.48-1984.

Manufactured in the U.S.A.

13   12   11   10   09   1   2   3   4   5   6   7   8   9   10

Contents

Preface

At its churchwide assembly in 2007, the Evangelical Lutheran Church in America affirmed the centrality of the Bible to Christian life and faith while at the same time recognizing the reality of biblical illiteracy in the church. The result is Book of Faith—a five-year initiative with "the goal of raising to a new level this church's individual and collective engagement with the Bible and its teaching, yielding greater biblical fluency and a more profound appreciation of Lutheran principles and approaches for the use of Scripture." *Book of Faith Lenten Journey: Marks of the Christian* is one of many resources prepared to accomplish this goal.

According to the Book of Faith initiative's Web site, www.bookoffaith.org:

> The Book of Faith initiative invites the whole church to become more fluent in the first language of faith, the language of Scripture, in order that we might live into our calling as a people renewed, enlivened, empowered and sent by the Word.
>
> The Bible is the written Word of God that creates and nurtures faith through the work of the Holy Spirit and points us to Christ, the incarnate Word and center of our faith. The Bible invites us into a relationship with God, making demands on our lives and promising us life in Christ. The Bible tells the stories of people living their faith over the centuries and, through its demands and promises, forms us as a people of faith.
>
> The language of the Bible becomes our language. It shapes how we think and speak about God, about the world, and about ourselves. We become renewed, enlivened, and empowered as the language of Scripture forms our hearts, our minds, our community conversation, and our commitments.

Book of Faith Lenten Journey: Marks of the Christian will lead you into an encounter with God through a slow, prayerful reflection upon Romans 12:1-15. The primary goal is not to fill your mind with ideas about what the apostle Paul is saying in these verses. That blessing will come to those who take the time to read, reflect, and pray with the pages that follow. However, a greater grace awaits you. Meditating on Paul's words will lead you into deeper intimacy with the One who has known and loved you since before the dawn of time. The Spirit of Christ breathed the apostle's message and will breathe life fresh and full into you as you meditate on God's mercy and call in your life. That's God's promise, and God will keep it.

You can use this book on your own, with a spiritual friend or small group, or with the entire congregation. Worship helps and sermon starters for Sundays and Wednesday evenings in Lent are available online at www.bookoffaith.org.

Be sure to visit the Book of Faith Web site regularly for more resources designed to bring the book of faith and the community of faith closer together.

Introduction

So often we read the Bible moralistically and legalistically. Our eyes fix on words that tell us what to do and what not to do, on what we have done wrong or failed to do. Read this way, the Bible quickly degenerates into a nagging kill-joy, pointing out our weaknesses and failures to be what we think God wants of us. It also becomes a book that is primarily about us, not about God—and what God, in incomprehensible love, is doing for us and all creation.

A theme like "marks of the Christian" could easily fall into this trap, devolving into a finger-shaking rant about the "marks" we should be working up to show we are followers of Jesus.

But "marks of the Christian" are not God's "must-do" list for our lives. They are God's work in us. They are what happens in a human soul under the impact of a love that knows no boundaries, a grace which constantly seeks and wants us, a God who has treasured us since before the dawn of time.

We are filled—marked—with the fullness of God (Ephesians 3:19) as immeasurable grace and everlasting love sinks in and begins to color everything in us with the beauty of God. And we begin, however partially and imperfectly, to see as God sees, to love as God loves, to hunger as God hungers for the beauty of the love of Christ to fill all that is.

We are changed and transformed as we participate in God's own life and nature. Martin Luther writes, "We are filled with God, and He pours into us all his gifts and fills us with His Spirit, who makes us courageous. He enlightens us with His light, His life lives in us. His beatitude makes us blessed, and His love causes love to rise in us. Put briefly, He fills us in order that everything He is and everything He can do might be in us in all its fullness, and work powerfully."[1]

Love changes everything. The Love whom God is remakes us in the image of the Love in which we are created, restoring in us that image so marred, so broken and scarred by sin and unbelief.

"Marks" of this restored image are variously described in Christian Scripture. In Romans 12, the focus of this Lenten journey, the apostle Paul gives us a partial picture of life transformed by the Spirit of God. Romans is Paul's magnum opus. In early chapters of this letter to the church at Rome, he masterfully lays out how God makes human beings righteous, showing the impartiality of God. All have sinned, but the love and righteousness of God are revealed and given to all in Jesus Christ. God has shown faithful love and kindness in Christ, and it is just this impartial, loving kindness and humility that is to "mark" us and our shared life in community.

As God is, so are we becoming, through the power of the Spirit within and among us. The pattern of Christ's life, lived for others, marks even our lives.[2]

The Way of Prayer

Our lives, then, are a constant struggle of the desires of the Spirit against the desires of the flesh. The Spirit of God wages pitched battle against all that disfigures and obscures the image of Christ in us. In baptism, we enter this struggle, coming to know that the Spirit is at work in us to will and to do what is pleasing to God (Philippians 2:13). Amid the struggle, we cry out again and again to Christ for mercy and aid. The battle we fight is best done humbly—on our knees, so to speak—in prayer.

This kind of prayer breathes through the reflections that comprise the bulk of this little book. Most of the reflections are written in the form of prayer, and all of them arise out of praying the Scriptures, specifically Paul's call for transformed lives in Romans 12. I listened to Paul's words, paying close attention to what God was saying to and in me. And I wrote as I became aware of the memories and wounds that were stirred by my meditation.

What hurts and hopes appeared? What blessings and gifts? What signs of transformation appeared in my life and the lives of the many souls I have met during years of writing, service, and travel? What questions appeared making me hunger for God's answer? What joys or anger at God, myself, and others bubbled to the surface of consciousness?

All of this, moved by God's speaking through Paul's words, became the substance of my prayer and of the thoughts poured into the written reflections. These reflections offer a glimpse into the prayer of one soul. They also invite you to listen prayerfully to them and to the verses from Romans 12. Listen to how God is speaking to you, drawing you into deeper intimacy with the Love whom God is.

It is out of such prayer that God awakens and shapes in us marks of the Christian life, which in fact are marks of God's own Triune love. Through such prayer we participate in the struggle of Spirit with the flesh. This kind of prayer is deeply rooted in the church's history. A glimpse of that history—and what Luther did with it—can transform our lives of prayer.

In Tune with Luther

When Martin Luther wrote *A Simple Way to Pray* for his barber, Peter, he called upon the church's deep history of teaching about prayer.[3] Luther was immersed in that history when he entered the Augustinian monastery in Erfurt, Germany as a young man. He would have practiced and learned more about the liturgical hours of prayer, with which he was already well acquainted. He also would have received instruction in a form of meditation upon Scripture that is known as *lectio divina*—divine reading.

Lectio is a form of slow and deliberate listening to God speaking to us through the biblical text. One reads a few verses or a story from Scripture. After reading that passage several times, prayer then moves to meditation—chewing on the text, turning it over in heart and mind, listening for what it stirs in memory, heart, and desire. This leads to a third movement of prayer, speaking to God about what is noticed in the words of Scripture and in oneself as God's speaking touches one's life. Meditating upon God's word stirs old hurts and fresh hope. It brings awareness of our sins and successes, angers and fears, memories and joys. Through it all, the Spirit of God, speaking in the word, seeks to touch and heal us, to make us whole—and call us into intimate loving relationship with the Love whom all the world cannot contain, transforming our lives into expressions of the loving heart of God.

A final or fourth movement of *lectio* is resting, just being in God's love, abiding in grace, not needing to do or say anything. Like an old couple falling silent in each other's company, we have said what needs to be said. Our hearts are full and at peace. In simple silence we can just be with each other, communicating not by words but in a heart-to-heart communion beyond the capacity of words to speak.

This is how the movements of *lectio divina* have come to be understood through centuries of prayerful reading of Scripture, but Peter, Luther's barber, would have had no training in such meditation. Like other sixteenth-century Christians, he would have known the *Our Father,* the *Hail Mary*, and other prayers heard at mass or taught for private devotion. *Lectio's* prayerful way of listening for God, however, was considered beyond the reach of common laity. It was for monks and nuns, the professionally religious who were "spiritually advanced."

Luther took the inspiration and shape of this centuries-old teaching on prayer and reshaped it, adding concrete directives and making it easier and more available for everyone who hungers to know God in prayer. Writing to Peter, Luther provided a primer that offers a deeply meditative and intimate way of being with God.

Luther invited Peter to read the text—whether of Scripture, the catechism, or other devotional material such as hymns—in four ways:

1. Read it as a schoolbook, reflecting upon what God is teaching you.
2. Read it as a song or praise book, giving thanks to God for the gifts God gives or brings to your awareness.
3. Read it as a penitential book, confessing to God your sins, your needs, and your weaknesses as they are revealed in your reflection.
4. Turn the words into a short prayer you may speak to God.

Following this pattern, even those with no training in *lectio divina* could begin to meditate, prayerfully taking in God's word of law and gospel, grace and guidance, listening to what God is saying to heart and mind.

The genius and core of Luther's instruction on prayer is the conviction that Scripture is not intended to fill our minds with interesting ideas. It is given to reveal the wondrous reality of God's unspeakable love and to invite us into trusting, faithful relationship that we might truly *know God*. That is, Scripture is given so that we might know God not as a pleasant idea or intellectual construct but as the living, Loving Mystery who is always for us, the one whose glory shines in the face of our Lord Jesus Christ.

Scripture is God's personal address to us, to the church, and to all creation. It is best heard—God is best heard—when we encounter God's word as a personal address through which God hungers and aches to draw us into loving intimacy. God yearns to know us, to be known by us, and to give us all that God is.

This is the faith and practice that informs and animates the pages that follow.

May your Lenten journey draw you into "the love of Christ that surpasses knowledge, so that you may be filled with all the fullness of God" (Ephesians 3:19).

How to Use This Book

Your 40-day Lenten journey into *Marks of the Christian* will lead you to listen to God's Spirit speaking in your own heart and experience. It will help you pay attention to what God is saying and how God is working in your life to heal, bless, fill, and shape you. It will encourage you to be honest with God about all that is moving in your heart and mind, *offering it all as prayer*. In this way, intimacy with the Holy One may grow rich and full, leading you also to love the world as God loves it.

You will benefit most by finding a regular time during the day to work through this book. It is easier to maintain a spiritual practice if you do it at the same time each day. Mornings are best for many people. The house and heart are still quiet and the busyness of the day has not yet distracted the mind. Others find that the noon hour or before bedtime serve well. Do whatever works for you to maintain a regular, daily encounter with God.

You will note that there are no readings for Sunday. The 40 days of Lent traditionally exclude Sundays, the day we celebrate the resurrection of Christ.

Although this book is designed to be used during the 40 days of Lent, it can be used at any time of the year. If you pick a time other than Lent for your journey, it would still be best to walk day-by-day through the book. This will result in a deeper experience that will mark your life with God in lasting and significant ways. It is also better to complete the journey than to give it up part-way through because you can't get it done in 40 days. Take a longer period if you choose. Set a schedule that works for you and be consistent.

Several elements comprise each day's journey, including great riches of faith, experience, and the witness of saints, mystics, and scholars. Sometimes you may find it fruitful to spend more than one day with a particular reflection, question, or quotation that stirs you. If one element speaks more deeply to you than others—blessing, challenging, or troubling you—spend time with it. Always go where there is fruit. Don't worry that the other elements don't touch your mind and heart that day. Go where Christ is pleased to speak and give himself to you. Luther wrote, "If you pause here and let him do you good, that is if you believe that he benefits and helps you, then you really have it. The Christ is yours, presented to you as a gift."[4]

Consider using a notebook as you work through this book. Jot down questions and insights, graces and blessings, challenges and changes in your life as they bubble up in you.

Each day of the journey begins with a brief reflection on a verse (or portion of a verse) from Romans 12:1-15. Most of these are written in the form of prayer, responding to what God speaks through the biblical text. Typically, several days are given to reflecting upon a single verse or phrase. Each day, the perspective changes, shedding new light on a particular mark of the Christian life. These daily reflections are intended to stir your own thinking and meditation, so read slowly. You may want to read each reflection two or three times, perhaps reading it aloud. Let the words sink into your consciousness. Take time to consider and benefit from what God is saying to and in you.

Following the daily reflection, you will find the heading *Biblical Wisdom* and a brief passage from the Bible that relates to the meditation. Read the biblical text slowly. Notice how it affects you, and jot down words, ideas, feelings, memories, and questions stirred by the reading.

After the biblical reading, you will find *Theological Thoughts*. These nuggets of insight, from saints and mystics, scholars and theologians, expand upon thoughts and experiences in the reflections.

Next comes the heading *Silence for Meditation*. Here you might spend anywhere from five to twenty minutes meditating on the readings. Begin by getting centered. Sit with your back straight, eyes closed, hands folded in your lap, and breathe slowly and deeply. Breath is a gift of God, the gift of life. Do nothing but observe your breath for two or three minutes. Focus your awareness on the end of your nose or your hands in your lap. Feel the breath (life) enter . . . and leave . . . through your nostrils. Each breath draws in God's gracious decision that you should live . . . and know abundant life in God's love.

Once you feel yourself settling down, open your eyes and slowly look over the daily meditation, the biblical text, and the theological nugget again. Note the words, thoughts, and feelings that draw you. Savor and explore meanings and implications for your life. Jot down any insights that occur to you. Do the readings raise questions for you? Write them down. Do the readings suggest anything you should do? Write it down.

Stay with the meditation time as long as it feels useful. When your mind is ready to move on, close your eyes, observe your breath for a minute, and thank God for the gift of life and for what the Spirit has shown you in your meditation.

The next heading is *Questions to Ponder.* Here you will find three questions on the day's readings. The questions use the insights of the readings to draw you into your own experience, so you may see where and how God is working in your life. Think them through and jot responses in your notebook.

Then move on to the *Psalm Fragment.* Here you will find a verse or two from the Hebrew book of Psalms that relates to the day's readings. The Psalms have always been a mainstay of prayer in the Christian tradition, speaking the deepest hope, joy, and pain of our lives.

Pray the *Psalm Fragment* and reflect for a moment before continuing to *Journal Reflections*, which offers three suggestions for journaling. Each suggestion invites you, in light of your experience, to reflect on a thought or experience expressed in the readings. Many of us don't really know or understand our thoughts and feelings until we write them down and look at what flows from the pen or through our fingers on the keyboard. We may be surprised to see what is actually moving and happening in us. Then we can draw insight and consolation from what God is saying and doing.

Journaling can be profoundly transforming when it is a regular spiritual practice. It keeps us more closely in touch with movements in our hearts and minds. It helps us discern what comes from God's Spirit and what doesn't lead to greater life, joy, and service. It may be useful for you to use a separate journal rather than your notebook, or to do your journaling on a computer. On the next page, you will find some suggestions for how to keep a journal.

The *Questions to Ponder* and *Journal Reflection* exercises assist you in reflecting on the daily readings and Scripture quotations. You need not answer every question. Choose those that draw you or move thought, memory, or emotion. Again, go where there is fruit.

Above all, be honest. Sometimes the most appropriate response to a question is, "I don't know." Don't hide your real thoughts and feelings (as if you could hide them from God). Offer them all as prayer, even when they are harsh and troubling. Such honesty is the road into intimacy with the Loving Mystery whose love burns for us and in us.

The final heading is *Prayer for Today*, a one- or two-line prayer to end your session. You might repeat this prayer from time to time throughout the day.

Hints on Keeping a Journal

Keeping a journal is a way of prayer. Journaling sharpens awareness of what is happening to us, lest we sleepwalk through our lives. As we notice and write, we respond to God with our thanks and pleas, our joys and sorrows, offering it all to God, seeking what insight and direction the Spirit is pleased to give. The process leads us into greater knowledge of ourselves and deeper intimacy with the One who loves us.

Consider journaling through this Lenten journey. It will help you focus and clarify your thoughts, while keeping a record of your insights, questions, and prayers. It will lead you to thoughts and awareness that will surprise you.

A Few Hints for Journaling

Write freely. Ignore your inner critic. Shout it down if you have to. Don't worry about writing perfectly. Pay no attention to grammar, literary style, whether you are writing in complete sentences, or what it sounds like. Just write! Simply get in touch with an idea, emotion, or memory and begin writing. Describe what you notice, how you feel, and how something is affecting you. From time to time, read back over your words to notice what is happening more clearly.

Be honest with God. Do not censor yourself . . . ever! Your relationship with God will be as real and honest as you are. Don't write what you think you're supposed to believe or feel or think. Don't write what you think is acceptable to your spouse or friends, your pastor, or your fourth grade teacher. Write your real thoughts, feelings, beliefs, and experiences as far as you can identify them. If you don't know what is happening in you, write your confusion and questions. These will open up avenues of discovery and growth.

Begin and end your journaling with prayer. Ask for illumination to see God more clearly, to notice what is really going on beneath the surface of your days and thoughts. At the end, thank God for what guidance, wisdom, or consolation has come through your writing.

Address God as you write. You may want to write your entire journal entry as a prayer. Share what is happening to you and in you, what you are noticing in your journey with this book. Like the psalmists and Job, hold nothing back. You will be surprised by what bubbles out of you.

Don't worry or stop if your journaling takes you in directions beyond the suggestions in this book. Go where you are led. Notice what you notice. The Spirit will lead you to places where you may drink from living waters. The journaling ideas in this book are suggestions for your writing. Don't hesitate to move in other directions when promising avenues appear.

Carry this book, your notebook, and journal with you every day during your journey (only keep them safe from prying eyes). Your Lenten journey is an intense experience that doesn't stop when you close the book. Your mind and heart will be stirred during the day. It is helpful to have your notebook and journal handy to write notes or new entries as they occur to you.

Journeying with Others

You can use this book (and I hope you do) with another person or with a small group. It is best for each person first to do his or her own reading, reflection, and writing in solitude. When you come together, share the insights you have gained from your time alone. Your discussion can focus on any of the elements of each day's journey.

Questions to Ponder is a natural place to start discussions with a group or spiritual friend. However, you might find that a section from a daily reflection, *Biblical Wisdom*, or *Theological Thoughts* has stirred you or members of your group. If so, start there, and let the discussion flow in the directions that are most fruitful for the needs and questions of the group. The Spirit will lead.

If you are working through the book with people you trust, you may feel comfortable sharing some of what you have written in your journal. No one should ever be pressured to do this, however. It should also be a ground rule that whatever is said in a small group stays in the group.

Always remember that your goal is to grow in relation with Christ and his church. You gather to learn from one another, not to argue or to prove that you are right and the other is wrong. Practice listening and trying to understand why your discussion partner or small group members think as they do.

Sharing your experiences is a way of encouraging and guiding each other. It provides the opportunity to offer feedback gently and to help each other translate insight into action.

By all means, pray together. This strengthens the spiritual bonds among those who take the journey together. Spend a few moments sharing prayer requests around the theme of the day. Then pray for each other and your faith community as you bring your time together to a close.

Journey Week One

I appeal to you therefore, brothers and sisters, by the mercies of God, to present your bodies as a living sacrifice, holy and acceptable to God, which is your spiritual worship. Do not be conformed to this world, but be transformed by the renewing of your minds, so that you may discern what is the will of God—what is good and acceptable and perfect.

For by the grace given to me I say to everyone among you not to think of yourself more highly than you ought to think.
      Romans 12:1-3a

Remembering
Day 1—Ash Wednesday

Vision
Day 4

Sacrifice
Day 2

Discernment
Day 5

Worship
Day 3

Freedom
Day 6

Remembering
Day 1—Ash Wednesday

I appeal to you therefore, brothers and sisters, by the mercies of God, to present your bodies as a living sacrifice . . .
Romans 12:1a

The morning comes, dearest Jesus, and I hunger again to taste your blessing. May the grace of all eternity flow through my soul, a river of peace, cooling my fevered life and the lives of all I touch this day.

May it be so, and so that it may be, I remember your mercies—one that changed everything.

I remember driving to Dubuque, Iowa, and parking in front of Martin Luther's statue at Wartburg Seminary. Sitting silently, gazing at the bell tower rising over the beckoning doorway of the school, I hungered to enter. But my hopes drowned in the awareness that it was impossible. I knew I would never walk through those doors.

A college drop-out, I made cheese, sold cars, and worked in a drapery factory. The longer I worked at each, the more I ached for another life, a life wrapped in the gospel of a love for which I had no words. Still don't.

Your love burned for me and in me, Holy Mystery. And I yearned for more, to know more, to feel more, to touch the flame of the love whose source is beyond human imagining.

Through the restless burning of my soul, you moved me beyond my fears to throw myself into the arms of the hope you ignited in me. Loving Mystery, you were—and are—that hope that burns in us, moving us to reach beyond the fears that hold us back from more deeply knowing and serving you.

Relentlessly, you stirred my restlessness, my discomfort, and I forgot how much work it would be, how much money it would cost, and how impossible it all seemed as Dixie and I planned for our first child.

And I walked through the doors beneath the tower into a new world, a world of study and service, of learning to love as you love. This is your mercy to me. You refused to leave me to my fears so that I might enter the hope you had in me.

The day begins, and I remember your mercies, just one that coaxed me into the warmth of your eternal embrace.

Biblical Wisdom
In the same way he took the cup also, after supper, saying . . . "Do this, as often as you drink it, in remembrance of me."
1 Corinthians 11:25

Theological Thoughts
Each person meets God in his or her own experience, whether that experience occurs with a community at a liturgical or paraliturgical service, or with one or two others, or alone. [5]

Silence for Meditation

Questions to Ponder
- What memories of blessings did today's reflection call to mind for you?
- When you have been helpless and hopeless, how has God broken through to bring you to a new day?
- Where or in whom do you experience the "mercies of God"?

Psalm Fragment
I will call to mind the deeds of the LORD;
I will remember your wonders . . .
Psalm 77:11

Journal Reflections
- Mentally walk through a recent day, noting the mercies that come to mind. Write about the impact these have on you.
- Christian life is *eucharistic* (from the Greek word for "gratitude"). In other words, we remember and give thanks for the giving of God. What is the connection between the Eucharist or Holy Communion and your daily blessings?
- What is God's hope for and in you?

Prayer for Today

Open my eyes to your mercies that I may see and, in seeing, enter your joy.
Amen.

Sacrifice
Day 2—Thursday

> *I appeal to you therefore, brothers and sisters, by the mercies of God, to*
> *present your bodies as a living sacrifice, holy and acceptable to God . . .*
>   Romans 12:1

I wake again into a world where you are, Loving Presence. Lighting three small
candles, I kneel and mumble my prayer. My words strain to touch what I feel and
most need.

May my posture be better prayer than words, a silent crying hunger to know
you, loving and near. In kneeling, I give myself to you. Do what you will with this
life. It's yours.

And then I remember Dimce. The front curl of his wavy brown hair danced
as he drew a mass of intersecting lines on a succession of paper napkins. We sat
in a café in Skopje, Macedonia, on a sunny April day.

Dimce was the business manager of an agency that dug wells in poor villages
in his country. But this day he was diagramming how he managed a river of
food and supplies from ports in Greece and Albania, through Balkan mountain
passes, to refugee camps in Macedonia.

Eighty thousand lives depended on the incomprehensible scribble on the
back of a napkin. And Dimce never looked up. He extended his diagram from one
rumpled napkin to the next, explaining all the while, but he never looked at me.
He was totally surrendered to a life-giving task that had become a holy obses-
sion. Holy, indeed, for preserving and nurturing life is God's work.

I think of him, my Lord, and so many others who taught me without having
any idea that I would remember them years later. Dimce did not give you part

of himself. He did not surrender some small pleasure to discipline himself or to identify with your sacrificial love, as we do in Lent.

He willingly gave himself to your life-giving labor of love for the world. A deep desire within his soul moved him—not some external compulsion or law.

Tell me, from what life-giving spring does this desire flow, fresh and free?

Ah, it is you, loving God. It is always you. Give me that desire. Awaken me each day to your mercies that I may be as surrendered to your life-giving ways as was Dimce. Would to God that I should glow with such beauty.

Biblical Wisdom
Live in love, as Christ loved us and gave himself up for us, a fragrant
offering and sacrifice to God.
    Ephesians 5:2

Theological Thoughts
The church of Christ is a fellowship of givenness, a communion of holy surrender to an inscrutable love that continuously gives itself to the ungrateful and undeserving—that is, to us. Only the beauty of surrendered lives will make a cynical world take notice. If the church fails to nurture such beauty, the world is right to ignore us.[6]

Silence for Meditation

Questions to Ponder
- What do you do each morning or day to put yourself before God, centering your life and attention?
- When do you lose yourself in your work, losing track of time? What is that like?
- When and how have you experienced the joy of sacrifice?

Psalm Fragment
Offer to God a sacrifice of thanksgiving,
        and pay your vows to the Most High.
    Psalm 50:14

Journal Reflections

- Name some people you know who are like Dimce. Describe them and their effect on you.
- When do you experience the desire to give yourself more fully to God? How do you respond?
- Today's reflection refers to posture as wordless prayer. Describe when wordless prayer happens for you.

Prayer for Today

Draw me into the joy of surrender to your life-giving ways, that I may know and become the love you are. Amen.

Worship
Day 3—Friday

> *. . . present your bodies as a living sacrifice, holy and acceptable to God, which is your spiritual worship.*
>   Romans 12:1b

Beauty converts the heart and awakens worship. The cardinal's crimson glory splits my vision, and you speak, Loving Maker, stirring my heart to praise you. An explosion of orange lilies sways in soft morning breezes, waving gently with each breath, singing silent psalms to the inexpressible Beauty from which they spring. To you.

I wish I could worship you as well as the birch tree that stands sentry over my backyard reverie. Four trunks divide from a single stump, thick arms splaying wide, branches stretching high. They open their hands, reaching for infinite wonder, fingers straining to touch an endless blue sky.

In every season the birch tree praises you, Holy One. Bare in the winter, groaning in bitter winds, spring rains awaken a million matchless leaves transforming from green to gold and brown in due season. The tree's worship is constant, not separated out for a special hour or two set aside for you. With outstretched arms, it receives each moment as gift, lauding you as the Maker of the morning, glorifying you for the sterling blues and steel grays birthed with each new dawn. Day by day, it thanks you. Night after night it stands watch, in silent rhythm with the slightest breeze of your unceasing creativity.

It knows without knowing that praising you for the wonder of life, glorifying you for the smallest mercies, is why we are here. In this we find our joy.

May I be so wise, Loving Mystery. Teach me to live every moment as an act of worship, receiving what the day brings not with mumbling but as invitation to serve and praise you.

I have seen souls who know what the birch tree knows. With tender reverence, their minds, hands, and hearts receive whatever comes. They are mindful. They know. Every created thing is holy. Each moment is an invitation to worship you who create lovingly and love all you create.

These souls know what life is. Their worship rises before you, the incense of reverent hearts and loving lives.

Biblical Wisdom
But the hour is coming, and is now here, when the true worshipers will worship the Father in spirit and truth.
John 4:23

Theological Thoughts
If I am supposed to hoe a garden or make a table, then I will be obeying God if I am true to the task I am performing. To do the work carefully and well, with love and respect for the nature of my task and with due attention to its purpose, is to unite myself to God's will in my work.[7]

Silence for Meditation

Questions to Ponder
- What moves a spirit of worship in you? Where does God speak to you most powerfully?
- What elements of worship with others move or impede your praise of God?
- When is your work your worship?

Psalm Fragment
The heavens are telling the glory of God;
    and the firmament proclaims his handiwork.
Day to day pours forth speech,
    and night to night declares knowledge.
There is no speech, nor are there words . . .
    yet their voice goes out through all the earth.
    Psalm 19:1-4a

Journal Reflections

- Describe an experience of being spontaneously moved to praise God.
- Describe someone who lives with loving reverence. What does this person move in you?
- How has an experience of worship touched you or changed your life?

Prayer for Today

Make my life a living prayer. Mindful of your beauty, may I worship you in all things. Amen.

Vision
Day 4—Saturday

Do not be conformed to this world, but be transformed by the renewal of your minds . . .
    Romans 12:2a

Make my mind new, Giver of sight. My eyes ache for your holy future. I weary of the reality of the daily paper. I need to see a new age, the beauty of your kingdom.

Even now tender shoots of tomorrow push through the coarse crust of today. But my eyes are tuned to discord and ugliness, failure and suspicion, distrust and conflict, hurt and intrigue. So I fail to see where you are making things new.

And I can no more transform my vision than I can teach myself to fly. Yet flying is exactly what you made us for. You fashioned our hearts to soar and sing and know the freedom of living in a world where your loving is constant and near. We are made to lean close to catch the faintest whispers of your loving rule amid the din of the daily.

But I continually fall back into old patterns of seeing that are conformed to the hopeless vision of those who doubt your loving nearness, to say nothing of your desire to lift our hearts to flight.

So I turn again and again, seeking transformation of mind and vision. Blessed Jesus, you call us to repent and believe God's kingdom has come near. I need to repent. But I cannot. The Greek words standing behind the word "repent" mean "beyond" and "mind."

"Go beyond the mind that you have," you command. "Go beyond the mind that cannot believe and see the arrival of God's rule here and now."

Only you can transform our minds, dear Friend, so repentance is always a gift of grace. The miracle happens each time we see the beauty of your love, each time we are touched by grace and care, each time we are swept up in the joy of your grace-filled future.

Your kingdom comes in every act of grace, every gift of love, and every moment of beauty, transforming our minds to see beyond the cynicism of the present age.

Biblical Wisdom
"The time is fulfilled, and the kingdom of God has come near; repent, and believe the good news."
Mark 1:15

Theological Thoughts
The English word "repent" has a moralizing overtone, suggesting a change in behavior or action, whereas Jesus' term seems to be hinting at a change at a far more fundamental level of one's being. Jesus urges his listeners to change their way of knowing, their way of perceiving and grasping reality. . . . [A] new state of affairs has arrived, the divine and the human have met, but the way you customarily see is going to blind you to this novelty.[8]

Silence for Meditation

Questions to Ponder

- Are your senses more tuned to what is wrong or to what is good and whole?
- Where do you see God's grace-filled future already present?
- Do you believe God wants your heart to soar and sing, free and full? Why or why not?

Psalm Fragment
One thing I asked of the Lord,
that I will seek after:
to live in the house of the Lord
all the days of my life,
to behold the beauty of the Lord.
Psalm 27:4

Journal Reflections

- What ideas and feelings does the word "repent" stir in you?
- What repentance is needed in how you see?
- Describe the beauty of the Lord and how seeing it changes you.

Prayer for Today
Giver of holy vision, transform my mind that I may see your tomorrow. Amen.

Discernment
Day 5—Monday

Do not be conformed to this world, but be transformed by the renewing of your minds, so that you may discern what is the will of God—what is good and acceptable and perfect.
Romans 12:2

You are not a good gambler, my Lord. By taking an awful chance on us, letting us discern what your will is, what is good and perfect, you bet the farm on a pair of fours—a poor bet.

What do we know of perfection? And we grossly exaggerate our ability to know the good, to say nothing of our desire to do.

But you know what we are and what we are capable of doing. It's there in the daily news, growing more personal and petty when we consider the self-serving, pragmatic impulses that motivate much of daily living. We are bound and determined to ease our way and make ourselves look good, or at least acceptable.

Still, you invite us to discern what is good, despite our narcissism and perplexity. You leave to us to find your will. Well, not quite.

You pour the Spirit of your life into our little lives, expanding narrow souls with the presence of a love nothing can contain. The love that fills every corner of the great soul of Christ dwells also in us.

"Listen to that Spirit," you say. "It's in you, too. Listen to my love, loving you. Listen to what makes for peace and shows patience. Listen for what is kind and generous. Listen for what gentles your soul and the lives of others. Listen to the love that frees you from narrow self-concern. Listen to the love that awakens desire of exquisite beauty.

"Listen and you will know what is good, acceptable, and perfect. Even now, the seed of my will pushes through the rocky soil of your soul."

I see, my Lord. Your will is not an external rule bearing down on me, dictating the good. It is the internal invitation to love. It is your loving Spirit poured into our narrow, narcissistic hearts, making all things new. Even me.

So teach me to listen.

Biblical Wisdom
I pray that you may have the power to comprehend . . . and to know the love of Christ that surpasses knowledge, so that you may be filled with all the fullness of God.
Ephesians 3:18-19

Theological Thoughts

And so we are filled with "all the fullness of God." . . . We are filled with God and He pours into us all His gifts and grace and fills us with His Spirit . . . . His life lives in us . . . Put briefly, He fills us in order that everything that He is and everything He can do might be in us in all its fullness.[9]

Silence for Meditation

Questions to Ponder

- How can you listen for Christ's love in your life?
- How do your fears narrow your heart, vision, and concern?
- What risks has God taken on you?

Psalm Fragment

You desire truth in the inward being;
therefore teach me wisdom in my secret heart.
Psalm 51:6

Journal Reflections

- God's will comes not as an "external rule" but as an "internal invitation." What memories, thoughts, and feelings does this awaken?
- When have you felt "filled with the fullness of God"? How does this change you?
- Listen to your day. How is God speaking to and in you?

Prayer for Today

Fill me with your gracious Spirit that I may know the mind of Christ, who is all good and all grace. Amen.

Freedom
Day 6—Tuesday

For by the grace given to me I say to everyone among you not to think of
yourself more highly than you ought to think . . .
    Romans 12:3a

Sunday morning, I stand and walk toward the pulpit, pausing briefly to pray before stepping onto the platform. My prayer is about the same every week. It's neither eloquent nor very spiritual. It would startle many to know how crude it is on days my soul is at low ebb.

"I am nothing," I whisper to myself and God's listening ear. "You are everything." The prayer has effect. I forget myself and speak of that unspeakable grace for which my words are a rickety vehicle.

And I am free from me—the greatest freedom of all. I don't worry about whether I am doing well or looking foolish. I am just there, in the moment, knowing that how I look and sound is of no importance. All that matters is that your grace, my Brother, is spoken, heard, known. Nothing else.

For a few moments I lose myself in you, dear Christ. I think neither of how anxious or awful or good I am. I don't think of myself at all. Only you.

I love to watch my son make music. He knows how to be in just one place. With no sheets of music to distract his vision, his hands deep in the keys, he is given to one moment, immersed in one thing, utterly unconcerned with anything but the glorious sound with which he is one.

His focus is the music, the joy in which you empower him to participate. Concern for self-aggrandizement evaporates, a thin mist of illusion burnt off amid the splendor of a holy labor. There is only the music. Everything else disappears.

Are you like this, dear Christ? Not thinking highly of yourself, you lose yourself in the love to which the Father appointed you. May I so humbly lose myself, this and every day.

Biblical Wisdom
Let the same mind be in you that was in Christ Jesus,
> *who though he was in the form of God*
> *did not count equality with God*
> *as something to be exploited . . .*
> *he humbled himself*
> *and became obedient to the point of death—*
> *even death on a cross.*
Philippians 2:5-6, 8

Theological Thoughts

There is no evil in anything created by God, nor can anything of His become an obstacle to our union with Him. The obstacle is in our "self," . . . the tenacious need to maintain our separate, external, egoistic will. It is when we refer all things to this outward "false self" that we alienate ourselves from reality and God. It is then the false self that is our god, and we love everything for the sake of this self.[10]

Silence for Meditation

Questions to Ponder
- When do you think of yourself too highly?
- What has God given in which you can lose yourself?
- What is the mind of Christ?

Psalm Fragment
I say to the boastful, "Do not boast,"
> *and to the wicked, "Do not lift up your horn;"*
> *. . . it is God who executes judgment,*
> *putting down one and lifting up another.*
Psalm 75:4, 7

Journal Reflections

- What is freedom from self ? How does it happen?
- How do you use other things or people to worship yourself ?
- How can you center yourself in God, who is "everything"?

Prayer for Today

Grant that I may find truest freedom by losing myself in you. Amen.

Journey Week Two

For by the grace given to me I say to everyone among you not to think of yourself more highly than you ought to think, but to think with sober judgment, each according to the measure of faith that God has assigned. For as in one body we have many members, and not all members have the same function, so we, who are many, are one body in Christ, and individually we are members one of another. We have gifts that differ according to the grace given to us. . . .

Let love be genuine.
Romans 12:3-6a, 9a

Contentment
Day 7

Gifted
Day 10

Connection
Day 8

Love
Day 11

Needy
Day 9

An Open Heart
Day 12

Contentment
Day 7—Wednesday

> *For by the grace given to me I say to everyone among you not to think of yourself more highly than you ought to think, but to think with sober judgment, each according to the measure of faith that God has assigned.*
> Romans 12:3

My anxious eyes turn constantly to the future, my Lord. I reach for a nebulous something, an unknown someday when my restless soul will fall quiet, fulfilled, at peace. But peace seldom comes, elusive moments that pass before I can make them my own. So I push on, quickening my step but with little clue about what my soul requires.

For years I believed the lie that achievement brings joy. I believed that accomplishment stills the nagging voice that badgers the soul in the wee hours of the night—or the afternoon. "You've fallen behind in the race," it whispers. "You're not keeping up. We expected more. You've not done what is needed to satisfy the soul."

I raced on further and faster, admiring the distance between myself and others as if pulling ahead made me more real, more alive, more significant.

But this lie imprisons the soul, blinds the eye, and destroys love and gratitude. It goads me to do more of *something* to prove that I am more than the needy old self that I am, more than ordinary, more than this soul so ridden with anxious fears about its adequacy.

So tell me Jesus, where is this rest you promised to those who come to you, who take up your yoke (Matthew 11:28-30)?

"Ah, it's there," your heart says to mine. "Peace awaits you. Look and soberly see what I have given you, gifts written deep in your flesh. Remember the streets you have walked, the faces you have known and loved, the sights and sounds that have filled your years. This is the measure you have received from my hand.

"You need nothing more to enter contentment of heart. Savor them all. Love everything I have given on your way. Turn from the voices that nag, and release your restless fears that you have not done or received enough. And don't worry what others may have.

"Look at the measure the Father appointed for you and stop running so fast. You are not ordinary. You are mine."

Biblical Wisdom
"Come to me, all you that are weary and are carrying heavy burdens, and I will give you rest. Take my yoke upon you, and learn from me; for I am gentle and humble in heart, and you will find rest for your souls."
   Matthew 11:28-29

Theological Thoughts
If you want to find rest here below, and hereafter, in all circumstances say, Who am I? and do not judge anyone.[11]

Silence for Meditation

Questions to Ponder
- What drives you to "race on further and faster"?
- How do you try to lift yourself above others?
- How are fear of inadequacy and arrogance connected?

Psalm Fragment
Gracious is the Lord, and righteous;
      our God is merciful.
The Lord protects the simple;
      when I was brought low, he saved me.
Return, O my soul, to your rest,
      for the Lord has dealt bountifully with you.
   Psalm 116:5-7

Journal Reflections

- In your life, how have you handled the lie that achievement and accomplishment bring joy and peace?
- What is the measure of grace and blessing in your life? Does reflecting on this bring rest to your soul?
- How does comparing yourself with others trouble your soul?

Prayer for Today

Teach me gratitude for the mercies I have received, that contentment may fill my soul. Amen.

Connection
Day 8—Thursday

[S]o we, who are many, are one body in Christ, and individually we are members one of another.
   Romans 12:5

The sun has barely risen and already my heart accuses me. Yesterday's failures drape the morning more swiftly than the spreading light. I failed you, my Lord, not to mention another human heart in need of a soothing word of hope.

I listened closely enough, I thought, to speak a word of grace to lift our common hunger for healing to you. But I tripped over my tongue searching for the right words to sing the song of our souls. And our hearts remained tethered to earth, untouched by the love for which we reached.

I know: Your love was there whether we felt it or not. But we needed to touch and know the connection we share with each other in you. Now I wonder if you wanted me to fail, if only to free me (again!) from crazy ideas floating around in my head.

So often I think that fulfillment of life is simply to know your love in secret silence, resting wordlessly in the sea of your mercy, sweet moments of grace. So I cut myself off from others, wanting to be alone, all the while fearing that if they stand too close to me for very long they will see my deficiencies, which I (and you) know all too well.

But the agitation of my failure tells me how wrong I am. The fulfillment of my life is not private awareness of the immensity of your love. It is to be connected with others in a sea of love that flows from one heart to another, connecting us flesh-to-flesh so that the illusion of our separateness is washed away.

Then we know we are members of a single body, joined in a common heart that is not our own, sharing that infinite love that ever flows from the unsearchable depths of your infinite heart, dear Friend.

Nothing stops the eternal flow of your inexhaustible love, a tide of mercy towing us home to each other in you.

Biblical Wisdom
The bread that we break, is it not a sharing in the body of Christ? Because there is one bread, we all who are many are one body, for we all partake of one bread.
    1 Corinthians 10:16b-17

Theological Thoughts
The *telos* or end of human personhood is received as a gift in the encounter with all those who invite us into fuller participation in the one and mutual Love, a relationality within which is disclosed what it means to be human in its fullness . . . to find and give the gift of self in the communion of interpersonal love.[12]

Silence for Meditation

Questions to Ponder
- Is your faith a "personal thing" or does it lead you to others?
- Where do you experience connection with others in Christ?
- How does Holy Communion show what God is doing in the church and world?

Psalm Fragment
How very good and pleasant it is
when kindred live together in unity!
. . . It is like the dew of Hermon,
Which falls on the mountains of Zion.
Psalm 133:1, 3

Journal Reflections
- What is it like to be "joined in a common heart," sharing an "infinite love"?
- How does God draw you out of isolation and into fuller relationship?
- Various words for God have been used—Loving Mystery, Friend, Lord, etc. Which words for God help you?

Prayer for Today
May the river of your love connect me with all that you love. Amen.

Needy
Day 9—Friday

For as in one body we have many members, and not all members have the same function, so we, who are many, are one body in Christ, and individually we are members one of another.
Romans 12:5

It's not a compliment, my Lord. No one wants to be thought *needy*. The word conjures up fears of being weak-kneed and wishy-washy, unable to stand on our own feet. We spend loads of physical and psychological energy convincing others—and ourselves—that we are autonomous, independent-minded people who know what we are doing.

I find more freedom in stating the obvious: I need. I need others' support and concern, their ideas and insights, their presence. I don't want to be alone in the labors of my life.

I need the presence of those who know what I do not, who have strengths I will never have. I need their companionship, their words, their touch, their laughter, their pains. I need them when I am uncertain about what to do—even if they don't know any more than I do.

I need the flesh-and-soul partnership of human hearts and minds, or I soon wonder: Am I alone? Am I on the right track?

I am not alone in this. I am . . . *average*.

My four-year-old grandson objects when I help him put his train together. "Me. I will do it." Already it starts, my Lord. His growing independence is good, but is this the first step down an awful and lonely road?

Maturity equals autonomy in our culture. The human journey moves from the dependence of childhood to the independence of adulthood. But is this all? I have known human souls so fixated on their independence that they lived malformed, sub-human lives because they found it embarrassing to *need*.

Needing implies deficiency and dependence, bearing the flush of shame. Is this why my first impulse is to refuse help, even when it is freely offered?

Again, I believe a lie, failing to see that I am made for communion with other human souls who were made for me and me for them. We fly into the grace of communion on the wings of our needs, sharing our varied gifts and tasting loving communion in you.

Your body, dear Christ, is a vision of human community restored. Amen.

Biblical Wisdom
All who believed were together and had all things in common; they would sell their possessions and goods and distribute the proceeds to all, as any had need.
  Acts 2:44-45

Theological Thoughts
All humans share the same basic needs, and even more specifically, the basic human condition is one of poverty—the most difficult truth to accept about ourselves is that we are insufficient by ourselves. We have needs that we cannot satisfy for ourselves—each one of us is dependent ultimately on the Other, God, who alone can satisfy the needs of the human heart.[13]

Silence for Meditation

Questions to Ponder
- "The basic human condition is one of poverty." What do you think about this statement?
- Does *needing* ever embarrass you? Why or why not?
- Where do you experience communion in Christ?

Psalm Fragment
I am poor and needy,
*   but the Lord takes thought for me.*
You are my help and my deliverer;
*   do not delay, O my God.*
    Psalm 40:17

Journal Reflections
- What needs draw you into greater communion with others?
- Is communal interdependence a countercultural value?
- How is your congregation a vision of restored human community?

Prayer for Today
May your holy church live in peace, a vision of your purpose for all things. Amen.

Gifted
Day 10—Saturday

We have gifts that differ according to the grace given to us . . .
    Romans 12:6a

What happens when your grace illumines a life, dear Friend? We come alive, often in ways we ourselves cannot see. We shine with the glory alight in your face, my Brother.

Your grace awakens unique graces in each life. Your light passes through the prism of our flesh, breaking into a spectrum of rays never before seen, never again to appear in the same way. And each gives you particular praise by being itself.

I remember a day, one day when I was able to say exactly the right thing at exactly the right time. I remember because it doesn't happen very often, and when it does it is a startling gift.

I spoke with Vincent in his dying. He had AIDS and not much time. Despair was all he possessed in any quantity. "It doesn't matter now," he sighed, "none of it. It has all been a waste"—his work, that is, his half-finished plans, his hopes for what he would yet accomplish.

He was only 33, and nothing brought comfort. No word of consolation split the gloom. No past joy awakened a faint smile. Impenetrable night shrouded his heart.

Cards and letters sat untended in a box by the hall closet. I began to read, discovering words of blessing and appreciation for what Vincent had done in his short life. Prayers and hopes for life eternal poured from pages packed with remembered graces, thanks for kindnesses, large and small, that Vincent had offered another human soul.

And right then I knew exactly what to say. "Vincent, if you had not lived, God would have loved the world less. For the world would have been denied that shape God's grace was pleased to take in you."

Your love is like sun on the water, Loving Contriver. Your grace plays on crest and trough, in light and shadow, shining a blinding ray here, a quiet burnished glow there—each an irreplaceable demonstration of a single glory. Yours.

So give us eyes, my Friend, to see the way your grace shines in the lives of all you love. And thanks for the grace of knowing what to say on just one day.

Biblical Wisdom
And all of us, with unveiled faces, seeing the glory of the Lord as though reflected in a mirror, are being transformed into the same image from one degree of glory to another.
  2 Corinthians 3:18

Theological Thoughts
God's dream in our hearts is a tender but all-powerful seed. . . . Day by day, prayer by prayer, lived moment by lived moment, we notice and respond to the constant encounters with the living God, and every time we do so, our roots are strengthened, and the Godseed grows a little closer toward becoming a unique manifestation of its Creator.[14]

Silence for Meditation

Questions to Ponder
- What grace is awakened in you in the experience of God's grace?
- Does seeing others' gifts move gratitude or envy in you?
- In whom do you see the "glory of the Lord"?

Psalm Fragment
Come and see what God has done:
  he is awesome in his deeds among mortals.
  Psalm 66:5

Journal Reflections
- How does God seek to love the world through you?
- Does seeing God's graces in yourself free you to be yourself?
- What is the difference between a skill and a gift of grace?

Prayer for Today
Gladden my eyes with vision of the graces your grace awakens within me, glimpses of your glory. Amen.

Love
Day 11—Monday

> *Let love be genuine . . .*
> Romans 12:9a

I cannot walk in love unless my soul dwells in you, Loving Mystery. So I hunger. I yearn to sink deep into the cloak of your embrace, to lose myself in the immensity of your grace, fully at rest in the place of your peace.

For my soul is not free. I seek myself in every circumstance, depending on others' good words to buoy my heart and remind me that I have worth.

With bruising regularity, life reminds me that I am not okay. My best efforts are often not wanted or welcome, and shouldn't be. Others reject or remain indifferent, and the soul plummets. And I judge myself—wanting, irretrievably flawed, seeking comfort from those willing to salve a fragile ego.

I cannot love, not really, not freely, and love must be free or it is not love. I am a slave as long as my worth rests in the opinions of others. Only when free from seeking myself in their judgments can I give myself in genuine care. Otherwise, I merely seek myself, living the illusion that my identity rests in the minds of others.

That's not much like your love, is it, dear Friend?

So I come again to you, to sink into your embrace, to cleave to your presence, hoping to be enraptured by a love that won't let me go, a love that says, "You are mine."

If I can rest there for a moment knowing a love freely given, if for a single instant a flash of awareness pierces the darkness revealing that I am cherished and wanted, my empty heart is filled. And I am free from seeking myself, free from every bondage that enslaves, and free to love, to share.

I can offer grace even to those who think little of me, as you offered your life, blessed Jesus, for your enemies and the friends who abandoned you. Such love comes only in freedom. So let me taste your love, that I may be free.

Biblical Wisdom

"My Father is glorified by this, that you bear much fruit and become my disciples. As the Father has loved me, so I have loved you; abide in my love."

John 15:8-9

Theological Thoughts

And it is about this knowledge that we are most blind, for many . . . believe that God is almighty and may do everything, and that he is all wisdom and can do everything, but that he is all love and wishes to do everything, that is where they fail. And it is this ignorance which most hinders. . . . [It] is God's will that we have the most confidence in his delight and in his love . . . just so does he wish us to forget our sins and all our depression and all our doubtful fears.[15]

Silence for Meditation

Questions to Ponder

- When you are you free to love?
- What fears and needs hold you in bondage?
- Where can you abide in Christ's love?

Psalm Fragment

O God, you are my God, I seek you,
my soul thirsts for you;
my flesh faints for you,
as in a dry and weary land where there is no water.
. . . Because your steadfast love is better than life.

Psalm 63:1, 3

Journal Reflections

- How are you different when you taste God's love?
- When do others' judgments control you?
- What impact do today's Theological Thoughts have on you?

Prayer for Today
Wrap me in the immensity of your love, that I may love as freely as you. Amen.

An Open Heart
Day 12—Tuesday

Let love be genuine . . .
Romans 12:9a

Love draws near with an open heart, willing to be moved beyond itself and its own need. So it is with us, and with you, my Brother.

There were days you'd had enough. You fled the clamoring crowd, seeking quiet spaces to commune with the Holy Mystery you called "Father." Seeking respite with friends, you ran from those who needed you for reasons they themselves could not name.

But your escapes were interrupted by the rabble. You saw them, sheep without a shepherd, and were moved to care when all you wanted was a little quiet where you could hear your heart.

So tell me, Jesus, did you need the crowd? Did you need them to stir your depths so the depth of all you are might see the light of day?

Did you discover that there was more in you than you'd imagined—more compassion, love, and power to make whole—because what you saw in their faces moved you beyond yourself?

Did you need them to become the fullness of yourself?

I think so, and that makes you just like me, Jesus, so human, needing others to discover the love which God pours into us.

Sometimes I find freedom to love in solitude and silent wonder, resting in your nearness. At other moments, I enter your love more fully in engagement as I see the suffering of the world.

A husband confesses his lack of faith in the face of his wife's cancer. An old soul names a long-ago affair that began as a way to assuage the pain of abuse.

A homeless woman asks me for a handout. A father seeks prayer for healing because he wants to live to see his children grow up.

Each moves me beyond myself, beyond my insularity, beyond my craving for quiet, to a compassion that is, well, beyond me. For it is your compassion, Jesus. And for a moment, I taste what is in you.

Biblical Wisdom
[Jesus] said to them, "Come away to a deserted place all by yourselves and rest a while." . . . As he went ashore, he saw a great crowd; and he had compassion for them, because they were like sheep without a shepherd.
Mark 6:31, 34

Theological Thoughts
Love is the *goal* of the Christian life. . . . [I]f I am a loving spouse, I *feel* love for my husband, but that feeling provides no basis for a marriage unless, along with it, is a habitual attitude of heart that wishes for and seeks to provide for his well-being in concrete acts of kindness, consideration, and service, . . . in small ways as well as large ways. . . . Love is a way of seeing habitually and responding to the real, separate, individual needs of each of the people we encounter in our lives every single day.[16]

Silence for Meditation

Questions to Ponder
- How is the balance of solitude and engagement in your life?
- What opens your heart to care?
- Where do you find solitude?

Psalm Fragment
Truly the eye of the LORD is on those who fear him.
on those who hope in his steadfast love,
to deliver their soul from death.
and to keep them alive in famine.
Psalm 33:18-19

Journal Reflections

- Did Jesus need others to become fully himself ? Explain your answer.
- What moves you to love, solitude, or engagement?
- Love is a feeling and a habitual attitude. How do feeling and attitude connect?

Prayer for Today

Open my eyes and move me beyond myself. Amen.

Journey Week Three

. . . hate what is evil, hold fast to what is good; love one another with mutual affection; outdo one another in showing honor. Do not lag in zeal . . .

Romans 12:9b-11a

Hate
Day 13

Affection and Honor
Day 16

Hatred of Division
Day 14

Zeal
Day 17

Seeking the Good
Day 15

Desire
Day 18

Hate
Day 13—Wednesday

> *. . . hate what is evil . . .*
> Romans 12:9b

Our loves create our hatreds, Holy One. Our hate reveals what we love.

I love my father, Lord. I love him even more as I remember the decades of struggle that brought, finally, blessed release into the immensity of your mercy. But my love makes me hate.

I hate all that polio did to him, wearing and weathering him until there was nothing left but a hollow shell crying out for the familiar presence of my mother. At the end, there was nothing but loneliness and the aching hunger not to be forgotten.

I hate polio. I wept and rejoiced when I read that the last case—the very last case of polio on earth—would occur in Africa at the turn of the 21st century. I wanted to go to the place where the last case occurred. I wanted to dig a grave and erect a marker that said, "Here lies polio."

And I wanted to dance on its grave. I wanted to mock and taunt it, sing sarcastic songs of victory, and tell it to go to whatever hell from which it came.

My hate was strong. Strong as my love. And I thank you for both the love and the hate.

But reports of polio's demise proved premature. It rose from its deathbed as my father could not, still to stalk the earth stealing and disfiguring lives that you love, dear Friend, even more than I love my father.

I have seldom thought of you as hating, but how greatly you must hate. How completely you must despise all that distorts the beauty and goodness of all that you so lovingly create.

You are life, taking joy in bringing beautiful beings to life and fullness. You delight in life, hating all that threatens, disfigures, and destroys the wonder of life.

So thank you for teaching me to hate polio. Thank you for my abiding hatred of all the hunger and suffering I have witnessed in my travels. Such hatred is a share in your life, a participation in your love. Transform my hate into action for the world you so love.

Biblical Wisdom
When this perishable body puts on imperishability, and this mortal body
puts on immortality, then the saying that has been written will be fulfilled:
> *"Death has been swallowed up in victory."*
> *"Where, O death, is your victory?"*
> *Where, O death, is your sting?"*

1 Corinthians 15:54-55

Theological Thoughts

For the Holy Spirit is the source of life and brings life into the world—whole life, full life, unhindered, indestructible, *everlasting* life. The creative and life-giving Spirit of God already brings this eternally living life here and now. . . . The sending of the Holy Spirit is the revelation of God's indestructible affirmation of life and his marvelous *joy* in life. . . . For us today that means . . . we have to build up a universal "culture of life" and resist "the barbarism of death."[17]

Silence for Meditation

Questions to Ponder

- What loves move your hate?
- How do you feel when you think of God hating?
- When was Jesus angry?

Psalm Fragment
The LORD loves those who hate evil;
> *he guards the lives of his faithful;*
> *he rescues them from the hand of the wicked.*

Psalm 97:10

Journal Reflections

- What thoughts does the reflection stir?
- How are love and hate connected for you?
- When in your life has hatred been a gift of the Spirit?

Prayer for Today
Stir my hate, that I may resist the barbarism of death. Amen.

Hatred of Division
Day 14—Thursday

> *. . . hate what is evil . . .*
> Romans 12:9b

Such an ugly word— *hate*. I recoil from it. I have seen the ravages of hatred on bodies and souls. I shrink from faces contorted by the will to destroy. They are a mask of hell, defacing the beauty of your image, Holy One.

I shrink from hatred's incendiary flame because if you command me to hate, that means *you* can hate. And I fear that you might hate me. It freezes my heart stone cold, for there are hateful things in me, secret sins and hidden motives I so easily despise in others.

I need you to be love—and to love me. And you are love. But loving means hating that which is not love, resisting it as fiercely as a mother protects her child.

And so you hate the powers that resist your loving will. You are drawing all the whirling elements of the universe into one loving union, a harmonious communion of flesh and Spirit, of Creator with the created. All that is will be one, a portrait of peace in which your love infuses all that is—and all that is beats in perfect time with the rhythm of your divine compassion, as in my brother Jesus.

Your church draws the richness of human diversity into one body, a portrait of a world restored, revealing your determined desire. We would do that more fully, dear Friend, if we only learned to hate the right things, instead of each other.

I usually hate the wrong things. I hate those who criticize and threaten my sense of competence, making me feel small or weak; who question my good will or judgment, complicating my life. I should thank you for them, for once I get over my frustration, they turn me back to you.

Better to resist all that breaks the bonds of need and connectedness through which you draw us to each other. Better to hate love's enemies that tear the fabric of the blessed oneness you are weaving out of us . . . and all that is.

Biblical Wisdom
With all wisdom and insight he has made known to us the mystery of his will, according to his good pleasure that he set forth in Christ, as a plan for the fullness of time, to gather up all things in him.
    Ephesians 1:8-10a

Theological Thoughts
God is continually doing his one action which is the universe. Hence, God is always active, always doing the same thing. . . . Christians believe that God has revealed his intention. God, it seems, creates this universe to invite all persons to enter the community of the life of the Trinity, the perfect communion of Father, Son, and Holy Spirit. . . . God wants all persons to live as sisters and brothers of Jesus in harmony with the whole created universe.[18]

Silence for Meditation

Questions to Ponder
- What images does the word "hate" evoke?
- Have you feared God's hatred? Why or why not?
- Do you hate the right things?

Psalm Fragment
Do I not hate those who hate you, O Lord?
        And do I not loathe those who rise up against you?
I hate them with a perfect hatred;
        I count them among my enemies.
    Psalm 139:21-22

- Where do you experience the unity God is creating?
- How does the church reveal God's intention?
- What does God call you to hate?

Prayer for Today

Move me to resist all that shreds the loving harmony that you desire. Amen.

Seeking the Good
Day 15—Friday

> *. . . hold fast to what is good . . .*
> Romans 12:9c

What is good that I should hold it fast, my Lord? Time and grace still my snap judgments. No longer am I as certain of good and bad as I once was. Things that I abhor become occasions of blessing and joyous tears. Opportunities filled with promise disappoint and sour the soul.

Polio rips through my family, shreds a promising future, steals health and land, leaving anxiety, struggle, and near poverty for my parents. Yet their struggle is the best thing that ever happened to me. It shaped my soul. It awakened in me the beauty of hope and the tenacity of courage. It stirred an unshakable conviction that life is beautiful and worth living, even when it is disfigured by events you would never choose.

Seeing their struggle freed me from false assurance. It stripped away the illusion of human mastery, and awakened a hunger for a grace that will not fail in the fire of adversity. It tuned my ear to hear you, Loving Mystery.

So tell me, Jesus, is polio good? Is disease a blessing? Is losing land something for which to be thankful? For I am thankful for all that those days have given me.

It is harder now for me to say when an event is good or bad. For your grace can make the bad into breathtaking beauty. And our callousness turns blessing into arrogant entitlement, draining gratitude and humanity.

So what is the good that I should hold fast? Blessings of your grace move me to tears— gorgeous mornings when the air achieves an exquisite stillness, light and gentle as heaven itself; the laughter of my grandchildren—of every child; the quiet faithfulness of those who have tasted hardship and still hope, trust, and love. All of these are near my heart.

But perhaps I should also cleave to painful times that remind me that life is not under my control, that flesh is frail and fleeting, that I am neither truly human or whole without help, companionship, love, and you.

So carefully I avoid all that threatens me and mine. Yet such things turn me to you with empty hands and an open heart, ready to receive the smallest of your graces. Anything that does that must be good.

Biblical Wisdom
Very truly, I tell you, unless a grain of wheat falls into the earth and dies, it remains just a single grain; but if it dies, it bears much fruit.
John 12:24

Theological Thoughts
[T]he love of God seeks us in every situation, and seeks our good. His inscrutable love seeks our awakening. True, since this awakening implies a kind of death to our exterior self, we will dread His coming in proportion as we are identified with this exterior self and attached to it. But when we understand the dialectic of life and death we will learn . . . to make the choices that deliver us from our routine self and open to us the door of a new being.[19]

Silence for Meditation

Questions to Ponder
- To what blessings do you hold fast?
- When has trouble become a source of blessing?
- What struggles have graced and strengthened you?

Psalm Fragment
I believe I shall see the goodness of the Lord
in the land of the living.
Wait for the Lord,
be strong, and let your heart take courage.
Psalm 27:13-14

Journal Reflections
- What memories are awakened by today's reflection?
- What is the good God invites you to hold fast?
- What death needs to occur for you to find grace and awakening amid pain?

Prayer for Today
Let me see your goodness this day, even where I least expect it. Amen.

Affection and Honor
Day 16—Saturday

. . . love one another with mutual affection; outdo one another in showing honor.
Romans 12:10

You call us to mutual affection, Loving One. *Philadelphia*, family affection, is your word. It wings me to a patio table behind my childhood home.

My sister, three brothers, and I sat at that table . . . and remembered. We drank wine and told stories about our father and mother, some I'd never heard. The time became a holy Eucharist.

Love danced and played about the table. Affection flowed deep and warm. Respect welled from our depths for the marvelous human beings with whom our very blood connects us. Stories streamed like a river. And we listened to each other with expectant delight, anticipating surprise, blessing, and heart. Seldom have I been so happy.

And never have I been more proud to belong to this family. I treasured every face at the table, and I thanked you for each of them and for revelation of your trinitarian life.

You invite us to lose ourselves in you. For you are the dance of love in time and history, in every place and moment—and most certainly at patio tables.

Warm waves of affection flow from the living fountain of your divine heart, coursing through and among us, inviting us to be carried away in the stream, finally freed from our awful self-consciousness and anxious preoccupation.

You are not some unmoved mover, solitary and untouched. No, my Lord. You are a flowing river of love, with neither beginning nor end. You burst forth, drawing us into the currents of your life, so that love courses mutually among us, from one to another, to a third and a fourth and back again, capturing our puny lives in your immensity.

Just so flows the love within your triune life.

Little wonder that you urge us toward *philadelphia*, an eager sharing of family affection and respect. For when affection flows among us, we know who you are and for what you intend us.

Biblical Wisdom
We know that we have passed from death to life because we love one another. Whoever does not love abides in death . . . God is love, and those who abide in love abide in God, and God abides in them.
   1 John 3:14; 4:16b

Theological Thoughts
To say that "God is love" is to say that God . . . is the life that pours itself forth: constantly, abundantly, excessively, never-to-stop-coming-as-a-gift. . . . There is often a deep experience of the Father as the originator and Pure Source of Love, Jesus Christ the Son who is the Love seen and heard in the Word, and the Spirit as the ongoing and inexhaustible activity of that Love, drawing everything and everyone back to the origin and end of Love in the bonding of Love itself. This might be referred to as the Trinitarian nature of Christian faith and experience.[20]

Silence for Meditation

Questions to Ponder
- When have you been swept up in love's dance?
- How is human affection an experience of God?
- Where can you begin to express *philadelphia*?

Psalm Fragment
Give thanks to him, bless his name.
For the LORD is good;
His steadfast love endures forever,
and his faithfulness to all generations.
Psalm 100:4b-5

Journal Reflections
- Which images of God (dance, fountain, stream, river, waves, current) speak to you?
- Describe a time of being caught in the stream or dance of God's love.
- How do the Theological Thoughts affect your understanding of the Trinity?

Prayer for Today
Grant me the warmth of your affection for those I meet today. Amen.

Zeal
Day 17—Monday

Do not lag in zeal . . .
Romans 12:11a

Love lives in deeds and dies in best intentions. And die, it does, my Lord.

Moments come when the heart wants nothing more than to love. Surging desire stirs me beyond the narrow confines of self to become the compassion that is our proper human destiny. But so soon my body weakens beneath a bad case of "*if onlys.*"

If only I had more time. If only I had more energy. If only it weren't so hard, so far, so expensive. If only I had more talent or had read all those books on my shelf. If only I wasn't so hesitant, so concerned about what others think.

Groups do it, too: If only we had people who were more committed, more generous, more willing, more open-minded. Well, then. . . .

A sorry tune, as ancient as it is new: "We only have a couple of fish and a few loaves of bread. If only we had money to buy food for all these people."

We have so little. That's the temptation—the lie—that haunts us, Abundant One. In a land of plenty, we fuss over what we do not have, a neat excuse for doing so little to love you and yours.

And you do what you always do, inviting us to bring what we have to be blessed, broken open, and given. You sigh and tell us to forget our self-protective "if onlys" and learn (again) that you are always enough . . . and always will be.

I need this on average days, my Lord, for my determined desire to serve you weakens in the heat of the day. Serving grows hard. Energy fades. Patience wears thin. People prove difficult, and I soon realize how badly I overestimate my ability to stay focused and give myself, even to those I love.

An hour ago my grandsons filled me with fondest warmth and affection. Their dark eyes shimmer with the fire of life and boisterous vitality. But they wear me out. By mid-afternoon, fading energy transforms me into a grumpy grandpa.

Again, I feel the frailty of the flesh and failure of best intentions. I need a strength beyond my own. So fill me, Boundless Source, that I may be broken and given for you.

Biblical Wisdom
Taking the five loaves and the two fish, he looked up to heaven, and blessed and broke the loaves, and gave them to his disciples. . . . And all ate and were filled, and they took up twelve baskets full of the broken pieces and the fish.
Mark 6:41-43

Theological Thoughts

How different would our life be if we could but believe that every little act of faithfulness, every gesture of life, every word of love, every word of forgiveness, every little bit of joy and peace will multiply . . . as long as there are people to receive it . . . and that—even then—there will be leftovers! . . . You and I would dance for joy . . . to know truly that we, little people, are chosen, blessed, and broken to become the bread that will multiply itself in the giving.[21]

Silence for Meditation

Questions to Ponder

· When do your best intentions fail you?
· What "if onlys" are your favorites?
· When do "if onlys" keep you from serving more fully?

Psalm Fragment
They feast on the abundance of your house,
        And you give them drink from the river of your delights.
For with you is the fountain of life. . . .
    Psalm 36:8-9a

Journal Reflections

· Does your desire wither in the "heat of the day"?
· What can you do to restore focus and zeal?
· Can you find fresh vitality in being "broken and given"?

Prayer for Today

May I ever trust that you are enough for me. Amen.

Desire
Day 18—Tuesday

> *Do not lag in zeal...*
> Romans 12:11a

What do you want? I ask, and the person before me squirms. It's always this way, my Lord, because . . . most often . . . we don't know.

So I keep asking the question of the parade of faces that come, now and again, wondering what is happening in them. What is this restless yearning for *something?*

"I don't know what I should do, how to choose. What's God's will for me?" some ask, as if your way is a riddle behind a locked door for which they have neither an answer nor the key.

But the answer is as close as their breath, though they know nothing of it.

So I ask again, "What do you want?" adding to their confusion. For they can't imagine that your will has anything to do with the desires of their hearts. They learned early and often that they are full of sin and nothing in them can much be trusted. Certainly, human desires have nothing to do with your holy will for us.

For decades I weekly confessed that I was "by nature sinful and unclean." I got the message. My desires cannot lead to you, only deeper into a confusing mass of selfish and conflicting impulses.

So we look away from the very place where you fan the fire to know, to love, to serve you. But you are always there, at the core of our hearts, stirring us to love some part of your creation and give ourselves to it so that it—and we—might live more fully.

We want to live, Holy One, not merely exist. And the life you have for us, the desire of your heart, is not locked away in a secret vault. Nor does it float among the clouds where we cannot reach it.

"The fire of my life lies within you," you whisper. "My holy desire is locked within your own. What do you want? Listen and live."

Biblical Wisdom
Therefore, my beloved, . . . work out your own salvation with fear and
trembling; for it is God who is at work in you, both to will and to work for
his good pleasure.
    Philippians 2:12, 13

Theological Thoughts
Late have I loved you, beauty so old and so new: late have I loved you. And see, you were within me and I was in external world and sought you there, and in my unlovely state I plunged into those lovely created things which you made. You were within me, and I was not with you. . . . You called and cried out loud and shattered my deafness. . . . You touched me, and I am set on fire to attain the peace which is yours.[22]

Silence for Meditation

Questions to Ponder
- How do you listen for God's guidance?
- How do you tell God's desire from your own?
- What desire to serve and love has God stirred in you?

Psalm Fragment
I will instruct you and teach you the way you should go;
I will counsel you with my eye upon you.
    Psalm 32:8

Journal Reflections
- Reflect on your desires today. Which lead to and from greater faith, love, and service?
- What do you want for your life during the next week, month, year?
- What distracts or prevents you from listening for God speaking within you?

Prayer for Today
Give me a discerning heart, that I may know your desire within me. Amen.

Journey Week Four

. . . be ardent in spirit, serve the Lord. Rejoice in hope . . . .
Romans 12:11-12a

Breathing Space
Day 19

Here and Now
Day 22

Aglow
Day 20

Hope
Day 23

Joy in the Spirit
Day 21

Smiles
Day 24

Breathing Space
Day 19—Wednesday

. . . be ardent in spirit . . .
Romans 12:11b

Bring me into a broad and open space, my Lord, where my soul may breathe the sweet air of freedom. No more doing, no more hurrying, no more flash and dash from one busyness to another. I need simply to be.

Perhaps then mind and heart can catch up with my body, and I will remember who I am, how I am loved, and what joy you intend for me.

Again, I come to this restless fatigue, tired of working, weary of demands on time and soul. Sabbath moments come too briefly, with little refreshment. I read distractedly, wander the house and yard, turn on the TV, but fall immediately bored.

With too much doing, too little being, I forget how to breathe, how to rest. The clock ticks inexorably toward tomorrow, and Sabbath too soon ends and I am none the fresher. The thought of returning to work repels the soul.

I want to run to a quiet place where my heart can cry its release and discover, at the bottom of its distress, a love staring me in the eye that was there all along. You.

I've been through this before. Each time I swear I will do whatever it takes to avoid coming again to this depleted place. But demands of the day and the drive of my anxious soul push me to fill the days beyond the limits of energy, to say nothing of joy.

I need to breathe deeply each day, or soon I am breathless, dashing in every direction at once, out of touch with the Source of my soul, losing myself—and you—in driven days.

But when I find open spaces to breathe, just to be, your Spirit is the air in my lungs and the exhilaration of being alive. My steps slow, energy returns, joy wells, and I smile.

I think you like that smile.

It is silent praise for the wind of your Spirit restoring my own.

Biblical Wisdom
Even youths will faint and be weary,
and the young will fall exhausted;
but those who wait for the LORD shall renew their strength,
they shall mount up with wings like eagles,
they shall run and not be weary,
they shall walk and not faint.
    Isaiah 40:30-31

Theological Thoughts
Our lives often seem like overpacked suitcases bursting at the seams. In fact, we are almost always aware of being behind schedule. There is a nagging sense that there are unfinished tasks, unfulfilled promises, unrealized proposals. . . . Being busy has become a status symbol. . . . Being busy and being important often seem to mean the same thing. . . . [Jesus'] call to live a spiritual life can only be heard when we are willing honestly to confess our own homelessness and worrying existence and recognize its fragmenting effect on our lives.[23]

Silence for Meditation

Questions to Ponder
- What experiences are stirred by the reflection?
- What drives you beyond your energy and joy?
- Where can your spirit breathe free?

Psalm Fragment
Create in me a clean heart, O God,
        and put a new and right spirit within me.
Do not cast me away from your presence,
        and do not take your holy spirit from me.
    Psalm 51:10-11

Journal Reflections

- What drains (or restores) your life and joy?
- "Being busy has become a status symbol." What do you think about this statement?
- What spiritual practices keep you "ardent in spirit"?

Prayer for Today

Bring me to an open space and breathe the Spirit of your life into my lungs. Amen.

Aglow
Day 20—Thursday

> *. . . be ardent in spirit . . .*
> Romans 12:11b

I love little children, Lord. Their eyes shine with the fire of life when they are whole and know they are loved. They glow with the elation of living, eager for whatever the next hour might bring. I want to gather them into my arms to hold and bless them, just as you did.

I walked through refugee camps in scorching heat, where there was little food and less hope. Children were starving; some sick beyond all recovery. The stench of death hung in the air.

But even there I found children not yet worn down by hunger and cruelty, playing, shouting, laughing, kicking a ball, savoring the sweet joy of being alive. Even in death's face, I found children who, miraculously, were still children.

They bring tears to my eyes, Jesus. I want to save them, and I need them to save me.

I need their glow to awaken your light in my heart that I, too, might shine with the delight of being alive, thrilled at the wonder of life pulsing through my veins, startled by the fact that life is—and amazed that I am privileged to share it. I want my eyes to shine as eagerly as theirs.

I grow grayer each year and a bit weary. Maybe it's inevitable that the march of the years dims the soul's inner glow. But days spent in refugee camps among the dying, the hungry, the forgotten, and the children tell me otherwise.

It doesn't need to be. I have seen your fire and joy in the most damnable places. I have witnessed the defiant beauty of those who live with hope in the very places human beings have designed to kill hope.

Every time I see the glow of your Spirit, my soul roars in defiance of all that kills body and soul. I shake my fist at all that destroys and disfigures the lives of children.

"There is something stronger than you," I exclaim. "Someone you cannot kill. And he is right here, in me."

And for a moment, I am as alive as the children.

Biblical Wisdom
Little children, you are from God, and have conquered them; for the one who is in you is greater than the one who is in the world.
   1 John 4:4

Theological Thoughts
[The] Holy Spirit is the unrestricted presence of God in which our life wakes up, becomes wholly and entirely living, and is endowed with the energies of life. . . . True spirituality is the rebirth of the full and undivided *love of life*. The total Yes to life and the unhindered love of everything living are . . . experiences of the Holy Spirit.[24]

Silence for Meditation

Questions to Ponder
- When are you as alive as the children?
- Name people you know who are aglow with God's life.
- What do these people move in you?

Psalm Fragment
Even though I walk through the darkest valley,
  I fear no evil;
for you are with me;
  your rod and your staff—
  they comfort me.
You prepare a table before me
  in the presence of my enemies;
you anoint my head with oil;
  my cup overflows.
    Psalm 23:4-5

Journal Reflections
- What does God's Spirit of life move you to resist?
- When do you say a hearty yes to life and its challenges?
- What does this tell you about God's call in your life?

Prayer for Today
Make me as alive as the children, even as you. Amen.

Joy in the Spirit
Day 21—Friday

. . . be ardent in spirit . . .
    Romans 12:11b

Moments of spontaneous happiness appear out of nowhere, Loving Mystery. And I smile, knowing who you are and for what I am made.

Spirit-breathed moments of utter gratuity turn up when I least expect them, thin places in the fabric of time through which your Spirit rushes in, filling me.

The little boy across the street plays, absent-mindedly singing made-up songs, unaware of anyone else. But I listen and hear the voice of eternity singing a love song just for me.

I stand in front of the congregation, broken loaf of bread in hand, a line of souls shuffling forward. Each face holds secrets. Some I know, and many more I will never know. Naming each face as best I can, I break the bread and place it in their empty palms: "The body of Christ, given for you."

For that moment, my mind and soul are undivided. Yesterday disappears. Tomorrow doesn't exist. Deadlines and workload flee the mind. All that is real is right here and now: The body of Christ, for you.

And a smile appears from a source beyond me, as if the smile is not mine but yours, Holy One. For a few moments I am privileged to look into those faces and offer a smile that radiates from the depth of your eternity.

I want to say to each one, "Don't you know? You are treasured. God delights in you and has since before the birth of time. Love unimaginable is here in broken bread and a bit of wine, a small taste of a great feast you will know. Just wait. You were made to bask in the warmth of the smile of God, present here and in the faces of all through whom the river of God's joy is pleased to flow."

But the line moves on. So I break the bread, say the words, and smile.

There are many times and places where the river of your all-possessing love passes through our lives, filling us with your Spirit. Aliven our senses to notice when and where your smile becomes our own.

Biblical Wisdom
[T]he fruit of the Spirit is love, joy, peace, patience, kindness, generosity, faithfulness, gentleness, and self-control.
  Galatians 5:22-23

Theological Thoughts
Contemplation is the highest expression of [our] intellectual and spiritual life. It is that life itself, fully awake, fully active, fully aware that it is alive. It is spiritual wonder. It is spontaneous awe at the sacredness of life, of being. It is gratitude for life . . . a vivid realization of the fact that life and being in us proceed from an

invisible, transcendent and infinitely abundant Source. [It] is, above all, awareness of . . . that Source . . . awareness of our contingent reality . . . as a present of
God, a free gift of love.[25]

Silence for Meditation

Questions to Ponder
- When do you have spontaneous moments of joy?
- When and in what do you lose yourself?
- Do you believe you are intended to bask in God's smile?

Psalm Fragment
You show me the path of life.
> *In your presence there is fullness of joy;*
> *in your right hand are pleasures forevermore.*
Psalm 16:11

Journal Reflections
- Describe an experience of being in God's all-possessing love.
- When and where has your smile become the smile of eternity?
- What spiritual practices help awaken contemplation in you?

Prayer for Today
Stir me to blessed awareness of your constant presence and love. Amen.

Here and Now
Day 22—Saturday

> *. . . serve the Lord.*
> Romans 12:11c

"Be where you are," my spiritual director once said. It's not easy. My mind easily flits among several places and a couple of time zones at once.

It's a common spiritual malady. We listen while thinking about something else. We work at one task while strategizing the next, fretting the past and checking our watch. Perhaps this is necessary to get everything done. But it fragments my soul.

We are everywhere but nowhere, missing the present moment, which is all we really have.

Ancient manuscripts disagree about the words in today's Scripture passage. Some read, "serve the Lord." Others say, "*serve the opportune time,*" which is this moment, here and now.

Lord, you tell me, "Look at what is right before you. I am present to guide and be served in every face and in each small task. The person and situation immediately facing you requires your mindfulness."

I want to make this point with a checkout clerk. He picks up the phone three times for indiscernible conversations as he processes my purchase and runs my credit card. With each interruption, he must remind himself where he was in the transaction, as I shuffle with growing impatience.

"I am right here waiting," I want to say. "Don't treat me like anything and everything that might be on the other end of that phone is more important than what is happening here."

My ego demands attention. I don't like being treated as if everything else is more important than me. But I wonder, Lord, do you have the same feeling?

Do you stand before me, looking at me, wanting, needing, crying out to be noticed? Do I miss you in the faces and situations I brush by to get to the next thing?

Truth is, I don't see you, and that's the problem. So help me to be where I am, for that's where you are.

Biblical Wisdom
"Sleeper. Awake!
Rise from the dead,
and Christ will shine on you."
Be careful then how you live, not as unwise people but as wise, making
the most of the time . . .
    Ephesians 5:14-16

Theological Thoughts
God still speaks today as he spoke to our forefathers in days gone by. . . . The spiritual life was then a matter of immediate communication with God. . . . All they knew was that each moment brought its appointed task, faithfully to be accomplished. . . . All their attention was directed on the present, minute by minute. . . . Divine action cleanses the universe, pervading and flowing over all creatures. . . . We have only to allow ourselves to be borne along on its tide.[26]

Silence for Meditation

Questions to Ponder
- What distracts you from the present moment?
- Where is God waiting for you to pay attention?
- How do you treat God as if everything else is more important?

Psalm Fragment
O that today you would listen to his voice!
    Do not harden your hearts . . .
    Psalm 95:7b-8a

Journal Reflections

- Describe an experience stirred by the reflection.
- Busyness is a kind of spiritual sleepwalking. What is your reaction to this statement?
- Practice "being where you are" for a single day and write about it.

Prayer for Today

Quiet my soul, that I may be where I am. Amen.

Hope
Day 23—Monday

Rejoice in hope. . . .
    Romans 12:12

What fans our hope, Holy One? Do we hope because of what we lack or because of what we have?

I remember the Dinka in southern Sudan. Many were herders of long-horned cattle. But when I was last there, the cattle were killed or as scattered as the people.

Civil war and gruesome atrocities tortured the region. Hundreds of thousands fled fields, homes, and herds, walking along dirt roads. People were starving and dying by tens of thousands. Small children, with hair bleached orange for want of protein, waited along road ditches to die.

Their pastors took bread from the altars of thatched churches and followed them, pushing ever southward, away from carnage and certain death. They set up altars under the scrub brush and celebrated Eucharist until the bread gave out, and it always did.

And the Dinka sang—hundreds, sometimes thousands of them—as they gathered, seeking the comfort of familiar faces. They had no hymnals, only songs indelibly seared in memory. One song lilted into the next with barely a pause as they praised and prayed with joy and tears.

"What are they singing?" I asked, and was told: "Death has come to reveal our faith." And I wept.

Death had, indeed, come. But it did not destroy them. It could only reveal the depth of their faith and the faithfulness of the Love who held them. Your love, my Lord.

How is it possible to sing in hope amid the hell of hunger and war?

Once I believed that the fervor of their hope was fanned by poverty. They had nothing. And nothing tempted them to seek fulfillment in what they accomplished or in some material good. Their sole comfort was to hope for grace and justice in a world beyond this one.

But I was wrong. The joy of their hope came not from what they lacked but from what they had. In faith and prayer—and certainly in song—they tasted a goodness and love that has no human source.

Hope thrived, for they knew a love that bullets cannot kill and hunger cannot starve. They had sampled your fullness and knew there was much more to come, whatever happened.

Biblical Wisdom

By his great mercy he has given us a new birth into a living hope through the resurrection of Jesus Christ. . . . In this you rejoice, even if for a little while you have had to suffer various trials, so that the genuineness of your faith . . . may be found to result in praise and glory and honor. . . .
   1 Peter 1:3, 6-7

Theological Thoughts

To have found God, to have experienced him in the intimacy of our being, to have lived even for one hour in the fire of his Trinity and the bliss of his Unity clearly makes us say, "Now, I understand. You alone are enough for me."[27]

Silence for Meditation

Questions to Ponder
- What fans your hope in God?
- What kills hope?
- What can you do to keep your hope alive?

Psalm Fragment
Bless the Lord, O my soul . . .
who redeems your life from the Pit,
who crowns you with love and mercy, . . .
so that your youth is renewed like the eagle's.
Psalm, 103:2, 4-5

Journal Reflections
- Remember a time when you lost hope. What happened? What helped?
- When have you known that God alone is enough for you?
- Has suffering stirred and refined your faith?

Prayer for Today
Teach my heart to sing with hope. Amen.

Smiles
Day 24—Tuesday

Rejoice in hope. . . .
Romans 12:12

"Are you optimistic?" asks the voice from my office doorway. "No," I say and smile. "I don't think it will work, but we'll be okay."

The subject of the conversation doesn't matter. What's curious is the smile. Maybe I'm just whistling in the dark, wishing for the best while expecting much less. But I don't think so.

It is a pained smile, understandable given the circumstances, but not self-conscious or deliberate. I have no time to determine how I *should* feel. The smile simply appears, telling me something more buoyant than my own melancholy spirit is at play in my soul, your Spirit, Holy One.

Despite the disappointment I fully expect, something truly good, even joyful, will come. We'll find laughter. And what's in me in this throwaway moment is much more than optimism. It's hope.

Optimism is a bright, brave face, pushing for the best outcome. It fixes upon favorable circumstances that stir sunny expectations. Hope isn't so cheery. It knows the things we fear can and will happen, but that's okay. For you, Loving Mystery, will also happen.

Hope doesn't look for this or that outcome. It wants you, my Lord. It wants to taste and see your goodness and presence here and now, amid whatever mess life hands us. Hope demands you and is satisfied with nothing less.

And hope smiles, convinced that the love that you are cannot be shut out of any circumstance.

Hope is you on the cross, my Brother, crying out, "Into your hands I commit my Spirit" (Luke 23:46). It is Grandma Dee, semi-conscious and half-dead, incessantly repeating, "I know what I am doing, in Jesus' name, amen," until she is finally at rest. It is the laughter of parish children filling boxes with food for the hungry in far-off places, food that will never go far enough.

Hope is handing ourselves and our best efforts to you, Holy One, knowing you will use them for your loving purpose in ways that we may never know.

But we know you, . . . so we smile.

Biblical Wisdom
Now faith is the assurance of things hoped for, the conviction of things not seen.
Hebrews 11:1

Theological Thoughts
It is God's will that we pay great heed to all the deeds which he has performed, for he wishes us to know from them all which he will do. . . . And it seems to me that this pain is something for a time, for it purges and makes us know ourselves

and ask for mercy. . . . And because of the tender love which our good Lord has . . . he comforts us readily and sweetly, meaning this: It is true that sin is the cause of all this pain, but all will be well, and every kind of thing will be well.[28]

Silence for Meditation

Questions to Ponder
- What's the difference between optimism and hope?
- When have you known joy amid pain?
- Who is a hope-filled person in your life?

Psalm Fragment
And now, O Lord, what do I wait for?
> *My hope is in you.*
Deliver me from all my transgressions.
> *Do not make me the scorn of the fool.*
Psalm 39:7-8

Journal Reflections
- How is Jesus on the cross a portrait of hope?
- Do you ever have the sense that "all will be well"? What stirs this for you?
- Where is your hope to taste God satisfied?

Prayer for Today
Teach me to trust that all will be well, for you will be here. Amen.

Journey Week Five

Rejoice in hope, be patient in suffering, persevere in prayer. Contribute to the needs of the saints. . . .
Romans 12:12-13a

Protest
Day 25

Prayer and Perseverance
Day 28

Patience
Day 26

Service to the Saints
Day 29

Endurance
Day 27

One with the Saints
Day 30

Protest
Day 25—Wednesday

Rejoice in hope. . . .
Romans 12:12

Tell me, Jesus, did you ever want to give up on the human race, chuck it all and escape to someplace, anyplace . . . simpler? It happens to me.

The morning news shows the happy smiles of soldiers returning from war. They are enveloped in tender arms. But family members of four missing compatriots look on through different tears.

A cascade of dark hair frames a pretty smile on the front page of the paper. She was 19 and preparing for a medical career. Her car was run off the road in a case of mistaken road rage. And all I can think of is the tears of those who love her. I am sad for the husband who would have treasured her, the children she might have borne, the patients she will never comfort. A waste of vibrant, wondrous life.

Tell me, dear Friend, is your love enough for this? Is there any redemption for this mess? Can any blessing make up for the senseless suffering?

And this is but a drop in the ocean of human pain.

So I flee to your church, seeking respite, hoping to find that there is more in life than the daily paper reveals. But even here I meet conflict, pettiness, and self-seeking—and a whole lot of people who are no more together than I am.

But then something always happens. You happen.

I listen and am touched by music of infinite longing and loveliness that speaks of a world beyond all sadness and tragedy. I am swept into a sunset, a burst of orange and purple on incidental clouds, painting an impressionistic wonder unlike any before or that ever will be.

Or I remember an old saint, blue eyes still clear and bright on his deathbed. He grabbed my tie and said, "It's time for *auf Wiedersehen*." Soon after, he delivered himself into your incomprehensible immensity, trusting—*knowing*—that nothing but grace awaited him.

And with all of this, I realize that I belong to a world more wondrously alive and beautiful than I can imagine, a world where even the daily paper will find redemption. Sometimes I see that world pushing into this one, promising that your infinite love will fill all that is. And I rejoice.

It's an act of protest.

Biblical Wisdom
He who descended is the same one who ascended far above the heavens, so that he might fill all things.
    Ephesians 4:10

Theological Thoughts

Hope is a trusting interpretation that the glimpses of life and beauty and glory in the present are not empty but full of promise. . . . [Hope] is also a response, a type of resistance and protest, against the presence of so much suffering, death and tragedy in the world. Hope must be able to face the whole of life in its ambiguous mixture of joy and grief, loss and creativity, suspicion and trust.[29]

Silence for Meditation

Questions to Ponder
- What kills your hope?
- What or who stirs hope in you?
- What spiritual practices help you live in hope?

Psalm Fragment
I wait for the Lord, my soul waits,
        and in his world I hope;
my soul waits for the Lord
more than those who watch for the morning.
    Psalm 130:5-6

- How do you respond to the desire to escape?
- What might you do as an act of protest against suffering and hopelessness?
- What graces lift you to hope and protest?

Prayer for Today

Awaken my hope in times of desolation, that I may lift the downhearted. Amen.

Patience
Day 26—Thursday

> *. . . be patient in suffering. . . .*
> Romans 12:12b

You are timeless, Loving Mystery. But we live in the meantime, between the appearance of Eternal Beauty and its completion. And the meantime can be a mean time.

I see you, Jesus, and I witness the wonder of what no eye has seen, appearing in your smile as you bless children, feed a multitude, and make human souls whole.

"If you want to, you can heal me," a man asks, kneeling before you. "I want to," you say. And I see from here to eternity.

Your face is a glimpse of the Eternal Beauty who brings time—and each of us—to completion, folding our little lives into incomprehensible love and being. Your smile reveals our final future.

But we live in the meantime. And seeing your beauty spurs dissatisfaction with what is.

Do you see what I see, Jesus? A young mother is diagnosed with breast cancer three weeks after her husband loses his job. A gentle old couple struggle with the man's mysterious illnesses and pain; one problem is barely solved before another appears. A beloved family member suffers through her last weeks of life. Cancer seems epidemic this year, Jesus.

There's plenty more: police and legal troubles, job loss and foreclosure, mental illness and declining parents, and long, painful recoveries. And these don't always happen one at a time. They sometimes come to a person or family in clusters, in combinations that I thought occurred only in country-western song lyrics.

Suffering comes to all of us. But so, too, the paschal mystery—the mystery of your suffering, death, and resurrection—comes into our lives. You suffer and are destroyed, handing your life over to the incomprehensible mystery of God. And resurrection comes. New life appears out of the end of the old.

"Wait," you whisper to our hearts. "Be patient and hope. New life will spring from the end of the old, beauty from the ruins of destruction, birth from the death of what you have been and treasured. That's the way *I* am."

Biblical Wisdom
Therefore we have been buried with him by baptism into death, so that, just as Christ was raised from the dead by the glory of the Father, so we too might walk in newness of life.
    Romans 6:4

Theological Thoughts
The paschal mystery . . . is a process of transformation within which we are given both new life and new spirit. It begins with suffering and death, moves on to the reception of new life, spends some time grieving the old and adjusting to the new, and finally, only after the old has been truly let go of, is new spirit given. . . .[30]

Silence for Meditation

Questions to Ponder
- What stirs your dissatisfaction with the way things are?
- Which story about Jesus most reveals God's face to you?
- When do you walk in "newness of life"?

Psalm Fragment
O Lᴏʀᴅ, you brought up my soul from Sheol,
restored me to life from among those gone down to the Pit.
Weeping may linger for the night,
but joy comes with the morning.
Psalm 30:3, 5

Journal Reflections
- What helps you live in patient hope for new life to appear?
- Describe a time when new life rose from the death of the old.
- How has your week reflected the baptismal experience of dying and rising?

Prayer for Today
When I am losing hold of myself and all I treasure, help me to trust that the deaths I die will bear me deeper into your life. Amen.

Endurance
Day 27—Friday

. . . be patient in suffering . . .
Romans 12:12b

I still think of her, Jesus, an old Irish nun, surrounded by dirty children dressed in rags. She lived with about 600 of them, gathered from road ditches and burnt-out villages, left orphaned or separated from what family remained when the bullets stopped flying.

A middle-aged man and some teenage boys helped her scrounge food from aid agencies in a Somali town. She tended to the children, keeping as many as possible from the field out back where 200 or so were laid to rest, delivered from the cruelty of war and hunger. A sun-bleached stone from the road marked each little grave.

The woman, beyond retirement age, kept moving, caring for a child or two at a time before moving on to the next group. Every day she faced an unending line of crying need she could never fill.

But she endured. She kept moving, and each victory was the life of a child.

Most of our challenges are not nearly as grave as hers, my Lord. Nor are the results of our labors so dramatic. But we are tempted to weariness. We may not face the physical and spiritual exhaustion of an impossible task, but we are challenged by tedium. We begin to believe that who we are and what we do matters little.

Most of our lives are routine, mundane, ordinary. Day follows day, and we go through the same patterns, attending to identical duties and boring details. We go to bed, wake, and do it all over again. It taxes the soul and erodes the will toward immobility.

As a boy, I mowed the back field where I played baseball. Standing at the near corner before pulling the starter, the great green expanse seemed to stretch to infinity. I could see the curvature of the earth at the far end. The job felt impossible, but every week I had to do it again. I didn't know much of life would be like that.

So tell me, Jesus, how do I keep plugging away with purpose and hope amid unending tasks?

I think I know. I think the old nun saw you in the eyes of each child. In the moment of caring, there was just her and that child. That's all that existed for her in the entire universe. And every task, every act, became an offering of her heart to you.

Perhaps that kept the line from looking so long.

Biblical Wisdom
Whatever your task, put yourselves into it, as done for the Lord. . . .
Colossians 3:23

Theological Thoughts
Unless a man say in his heart, "Only I and God are in the world," he shall not find rest.[31]

Silence for Meditation

Questions to Ponder
- What makes your soul weak and faint within you?
- What experiences have overwhelmed you and tested your endurance?
- When have you kept faithfully moving despite an impossible task? What helped you during this time?

Psalm Fragment
Hear my cry, O God;
listen to my prayer.
From the end of the earth I call to you,
when my heart is faint.
Psalm 61:1-2

Journal Reflections
- Does the old nun in today's reflection remind you of anyone? What do you notice about that person?
- Reflect on how every task can be done as an offering to God.
- What consolation or strength might come from treating each thing as if "only I and God are in the world"?

Prayer for Today
Teach me, dear Friend, the secret of holy endurance. Amen.

Prayer and Perseverance
Day 28—Saturday

. . . persevere in prayer . . .
Romans 12:12c

Once I thought that prayer was communication with you, Holy One. I prayed for this and that, graces and blessings, healing and peace for self and others. Mostly, my stressors determined the arc of my praying.

But something changed. I discovered it was not your graces I most sought. I wanted . . . simply . . . you.

And praying became communion, a simple, quiet knowing of you as the One who is love, the One whose love cries out from within my deepest heart to be united with the Love who is always beyond me.

You ceased to be a candy machine into which I fed coins, hoping to satisfy wants or imaginary needs. You became this unimaginable Loving Mystery for whom I hunger. And prayer had no other purpose than to know you, to touch and be touched by you.

Now, it is enough just to know the Love you are, to know you as the Love from which I come, the Wonder to whom I go, the Inescapable Presence whose center is everywhere and whose circumference is nowhere.

It is for this you called me into being: to share in the dance of love that is your life in time and space—and within my own life.

Words fail me, my Lord, for I speak of things far beyond me, beyond any knowing I pretend to possess. Too often my words suggest that you and I are separate and disconnected. But it's an illusion, a lie.

For you are within me, and I am in you. It is your Spirit that speaks within me, calling out for you whom I can never fully possess.

You stand—Spirit to Spirit—on both sides of prayer. And in praying, I simply stop and become aware of your presence within and beyond me. I know the truth of your life within this mortal life I live. Such awareness is truest prayer.

You tell me to keep praying, to stay at it. Don't let fatigue, discouragement, or your seeming silence discourage me. "Persevere," you say, "and you will have what you need."

I know who that is, Holy Mystery. So I bring all that I am, needs and hopes, pains and joys, trusting that you will give what I need.

You.

Biblical Wisdom
When we cry, "Abba! Father!" it is that very Spirit bearing witness with our
spirit that we are children of God....
    Romans 8:15b-16

Theological Thoughts
It is in this "Ground of Love" in which I am at all times, that I find my identity, my uniqueness, and my interrelatedness. Yet I can find [this] in God, *only if I am aware that I am in God's presence*. The task of prayer, then, is to help me to achieve this conscious awareness that I am indeed in God.[32]

Silence for Meditation

Questions to Ponder
· What are your most meaningful ways and places of prayer?
· Prayer is conscious relationship with God. Where does such awareness occur for you?
· How has prayer changed for you during your lifetime? Are there times and seasons in your prayer life?

Psalm Fragment
Where can I go from your spirit?
        Or where can I flee from your presence?
    Psalm 139:7

Journal Reflections
· Is your prayer more like communication or communion?
· Describe a time when you were simply aware of God, of being in God, of knowing God in you.
· Why do you pray?

Prayer for Today
I bring all that I am to you, my Lord. Fill me with all that you are. Amen.

Service to the Saints
Day 29—Monday

Contribute to the needs of the saints. . . .
Romans 12:13a

Dozens of things happen in a day, and you forget them all, then comes a moment that burns itself in memory and never leaves.

Samuel wounds me. I spent no more than 20 minutes with him. But I still see him standing in front of a small brick church in a dusty town on the edge of an Ethiopian desert. "Don't forget us," he says.

Samuel said those words, but I didn't need them. His whole being pleaded with me not to forget. Hands open, shoulders slumped, he was beaten down by what he and his little congregation faced every day in the marketplace.

They met distrust, hatred, and resistance from their neighbors and community, who avoided them, refused to do business in their shops, charged them extra, or gave them the poor goods.

And all because of you, Jesus.

They were hated because they named you the holy Lord of their lives—and of all that is. They dared to invite others to see the love of the Father in you and to bow in humble worship. Occasionally, they made a convert, which brought more hatred, rejection, and discrimination.

Yet they continued to witness to the suffering love of God that pours from your wounded side, your beaten body, your bloodied face—a face even more weary than their own. For you suffered then and now the rejection of those who can't imagine that you are the face of God's holy immensity.

Samuel was the pastor of this little throng, and he still stands there, pleading with me. I can't forget, but neither have I done more than occasionally pray for him and all who witness in places where it is harder than I can imagine.

He and his little band are so much more faithful than me, Lord. And as much as he needs me, I need him more. I need to hear his wordless pleading so that true passion may awaken my soul to love beyond mere words.

Samuel is the face of faith and love for which I hunger.

Biblical Wisdom
I have said this to you, so that in me you may have peace. In the world you face persecution. But take courage; I have conquered the world!
    John 16:33

Theological Thoughts
Passion involves a transformation in which love of others and the desire to heal, to offer comfort and hope, to persevere in suffering, and to offer forgiveness take on a radically new character. . . . [We] can return to love, and life, and service with new verve and feeling. The experience of passion wounds with the fire of love and opens the door to the utter fullness of humanity in God.[33]

Silence for Meditation

Questions to Ponder
- Who reminds you of suffering for Christ?
- Whom do you need to remember and reach out to help?
- How does the idea of suffering for your faith affect you?

Psalm Fragment
How long must I bear pain in my soul,
        and have sorrow in my heart all day long?
How long shall my enemy be exalted over me?

Psalm 13:2
Journal Reflections
- Where have you encountered rejection because of Jesus?
- Imagine Jesus suffering on the cross. What do you want to do for him . . . and his?
- Who or what stirs your passion to love and serve?

Prayer for Today
Blessed Jesus, show me what I may do for your suffering saints. Amen.

One with the Saints
Day 30—Tuesday

Contribute to the needs of the saints. . . .
Romans 12:13a

We are never islands apart to ourselves, Dearest One, even though we often feel that way. We are connected from the first moments of our existence in our mothers' wombs. You make us so that we might find ourselves in loving solidarity with others.

The saints know this.

The phone rang one burning hot Nebraska morning as I hurried to the car. Jim lay in the hospital, teetering toward death after a car crash. I probably wouldn't get there in time. But Magdalena, my caller, insisted that I wait for her to arrive with a package for "Jimmy and his family."

She delivered a long, late-night letter written in a spidery, old-lady scrawl. Scraps of paper filled a bulging envelope, each scrap scribbled with prayers and Bible and hymn verses—consolation for the dying and those who keep watch.

"I had to get this to him," she said. "He's one of my boys, you know. I had him in Sunday school."

That was long ago when Jimmy was a boy, not the spray pilot and mechanic he'd become. But the years didn't matter. He was still one of her boys, as I was. And Jimmy was my brother, as his mother was my mother, his father was my father, his brothers and sister my flesh and blood, though we shared no common blood.

Except yours, Jesus.

Magdalena, simple old saint that she was, had matured beyond the illusion of a separate existence. Jimmy's suffering was her own. His family's fear was her fear. Their struggle happened not in a hospital miles away but in the depth of her magnanimous heart.

And it is all because of you, my Brother. You join us, very different people, into one body united in a single heart, sharing a common bloodstream through which flows the warm blood of your unceasing compassion.

Any notion that we are separate individuals is an illusion, a lie that we live to our pain, perpetuating our loneliness and impoverishing those to which we are joined in your body.

We suffer pain at the points of our connectedness, Jesus. But the pain is never mine or yours; it is always ours. And in the sharing, your broken fragmented body is healed.

As was Jimmy. And like our pain, our joys are also one.

Biblical Wisdom
If one member suffers, all suffer together with it; if one member is honored, all rejoice together with it.
   1 Corinthians 12:26

Theological Thoughts
Love comes out of God and gathers us in order to pour itself back into God through all of us and bring us all back to [God] on the tide of His own infinite mercy.[34]

Silence for Meditation

Questions to Ponder
- When do you cut yourself off from others?
- Why and how is division within the church so painful?
- Who has reached out to you and dispelled your vulnerable aloneness?

Psalm Fragment
But as for me, when they were sick,
      I wore sackcloth;
      I afflicted myself with fasting.
I prayed with head bowed on my bosom
         as though I grieved for a friend or a brother.
I went about as one who laments for a mother.
   Psalm 35:13-14

Journal Reflections

- Describe an experience of oneness with others.
- When have you found yourself suffering or rejoicing with others?
- What does your use of words like "me," "mine," and "my life" say about how you see yourself separate from or connected to others?

Prayer for Today

Grant us an abiding awareness of our oneness in you, Loving God. Amen.

Journey Week Six

Contribute to the needs of the saints; extend hospitality to strangers.
Romans 12:13

Giving Yourself
Day 31—Wednesday

Contribute to the needs of the saints. . . .
Romans 12:13a

There's a large Bavarian cow bell on my office shelf. (You can wake the dead with that thing.) I accused my old friend Fritz of stealing it off a cow somewhere in the Alps of his native Germany. He just smiled. (Somewhere there's a lost cow.)

And somewhere there are human souls who are alive and thriving because Fritz lived. It could have been otherwise. Displaced far from home in the chaos of Germany after WW II, he was shot at more than once for stealing potatoes from farmers to stay alive.

He never forgot what it was to be hungry, scared, and on your own at 17.

Decades later he was a steel worker in Hammond, Indiana, a machinist. The Nazis had taught him well when he was 16, so he could help build fighter planes.

When the steel mill went on strike, Fritz fulfilled a lifelong dream to travel the world. On one stop, along a road between Agra and Jaipur in India, he saw two of the poorest, most bedraggled children he'd ever seen. He called them over to his car, reached in his pocket and gave whatever money was there.

Their eyes grew large as saucers, and they ran back to a ramshackle slum with open sewers and a single water pump that served thousands.

"Ya, vee got some trrroubles in the world," Fritz would sigh. But the world changed because of those two children.

Fritz went home to Indiana and didn't forget. He knew hunger. He knew fear. He knew what it was to be beaten down. And he talked to his congregation about hunger. He talked to church leaders about hunger. He learned all he could about what keeps people poor and hungry, then talked to state and federal legislators about hunger.

He was an old German refugee, stumping through musty basements of little churches and sometimes stopping members of Congress in Capitol corridors in Washington D.C. He helped raise millions of dollars for the hungry and forgotten.

There are people alive today because somewhere on the road between Agra and Jaipur, Fritz determined to give himself to one cause, one mission, one love, one Lord.

May he rest in peace, and may your holy angels—and two small boys—rise up and call him blessed.

Biblical Wisdom
Be merciful, just as your Father is merciful.
  Luke 6:36

Theological Thoughts
A brother asked an old man: "There are two monks: one stays quietly in his cell, fasting for six days at a time, and laying many austerities upon himself: and the other ministers to the sick. Which of them is more acceptable to God?" The old man answered: "If the brother, who fasts six days, even hung himself up by his nostrils, he could never be the equal of him who ministers to the sick."[35]

Silence for Meditation

Questions to Ponder
- Who, for you, is an example of giving themselves to others?
- How do our good works outlive us?
- How does painful experience teach us mercy?

Psalm Fragment
Happy are those who consider the poor . . .
The Lord protects them and keeps them alive;
    they are called happy in the land.
  Psalm 41:1-2

Journal Reflections
- To what do you want to give yourself for God?
- What do you want written as your epitaph?
- What joys have you known in showing mercy?

Thank you, my Lord, for Fritz. May I, too, give myself to one holy cause for you. Amen.

Hospitality
Day 32—Thursday

> . . . *extend hospitality to strangers.*
> Romans 12:13b

We are strangers, my Lord. And we are afraid. Save us from ourselves.

Dozens of people avert their gaze, avoiding eye contact, as I walk city streets. If it accidentally happens, most quickly look away. We avoid seeing each other, lest mere acknowledgement of another's existence make some claim on us.

We don't want to be bothered. Then we wonder why we feel so lonely or little understood. And we marvel about why society grows more suspicious, cynical, divided, and oh so bitter.

It's not that way everywhere.

A young Palestinian man walked across the cobblestones of Manger Square and greeted me. We were just outside the Church of the Nativity in Bethlehem, the place of your first holy appearance, my Brother. I tried to escape the conversation and be on my way, though I had nowhere to go.

"Where are you staying?" the man asked. My skin tone marked me as a stranger.

"With Mitri," I said. "Mitri!" he exclaimed. "I know Mitri. Everyone knows Mitri. His mother is my neighbor. Come, it is close. I will introduce you. We must talk, take some Bethlehem wine. You must come to my house."

I went, barely knowing how to act when another human soul opened space for me in his day, let alone in his home. We shared food and wine. Conversation became communion as we swapped stories like long lost friends.

And a great and open space opened up in me, my Lord. Comfort and laughter replaced suspicion and fear as I listened to lives so different from my own. Walls of language and culture crumbled. I felt human again, embraced, known, and welcomed, even as I welcomed another into my own soul.

It was sacramental time, laced with grace and joy beyond anything we brought to the moment. We shared a holy communion as you and your grace, my Brother, became flesh again, right there in Manger Square, for us to touch.

Such moments need not be rare. This is what you will do at every table, if we fight our fears and make a little space for you.

Biblical Wisdom
When [Jesus] was at table with them, he took bread, blessed and broke it, and gave it to them. Then their eyes were opened, and they recognized him. . . .
  Luke 24:30-31

Theological Thoughts

An ancient rabbi once asked his pupils how they could tell when the night had ended. . . . "Could it be," asked one student, "when you can see an animal in the distance and tell whether it is a sheep or a dog?" "No," answered the Rabbi. "Could it be," asked another, "when you look at a tree in the distance and tell whether it is a fig tree or a peach tree?" "No," said the Rabbi . . . "It is when you look on the face of any [person] and can see . . . your brother [or sister]. Because if you cannot do this, then no matter what time it is, it is still night."[36]

Silence for Meditation

Questions to Ponder
- Where do you regularly engage in hospitality?
- How might hospitality be a spiritual discipline for you?
- Why do you avoid receiving hospitality?

Psalm Fragment
O Lord, you will hear the desire of the meek . . .
>*to do justice for the orphan and the oppressed,*
>*so that those from earth may strike terror no more.*
Psalm 10:17-18

Journal Reflections
- What does receiving hospitality move in you?
- Why is sharing food so central to hospitality?
- Where has God become flesh for you, as in the reflection?

Prayer for Today
May I taste and be your welcome at every table I share. Amen.

Seeing the Familiar Stranger
Day 33—Friday

. . . extend hospitality to strangers.
Romans 12:13b

Many times I have eaten the food of the poor and have been embarrassed. And each time you were teaching me, my Lord.

After a long worship service in San Salvador, families competed with others to share their table. They wanted to ready us for our journey. I went and ate the greasiest, stringiest chicken I've ever seen, while our hosts looked on, taking more joy in our eating than in their own.

This was likely the only time they would eat meat all week. I was eating their very best, which they needed far more than I did.

It happened again at Cocodrillo in Cuba, a meal of sea bass, freshly speared in the bay. And there was a wedding feast in Ethiopia, dining on fresh vegetables, fruit, and goat, with coffee just roasted beneath the trees. In Nigeria we ate cassava root and mystery meat amid great heat and quiet laughter.

The food changed with each place and the faces sitting around on the ground were different colors and spoke various tongues. But the language of hospitality was always the same.

I should have been feeding them, caring for them, and in a way I was. I received their giving with thanks, fulfilling their joy in sharing with one who was richer than they could imagine—and also so much poorer.

For I didn't see the way they see. They looked at me and saw you, Jesus. I was a stranger to be welcomed, and in the welcoming we received your holy presence.

I deserved no such treatment. I'm just a guy who is making up his life as he goes along, who wishes he were less selfish, more giving, more committed, and certainly more clear about who he is and what he should do. But I was welcomed as you.

They looked at me and saw a familiar stranger, the mystery of divine presence waiting to be revealed. In their welcome, the marriage of your eternal word and human flesh happened among us. Host and guest together knew you, the One who is always waiting to be welcomed.

Biblical Wisdom
Do not neglect to show hospitality to strangers, for by doing that some have entertained angels without knowing it.
Hebrews 13:2

Theological Thoughts
All guests who present themselves are to be welcomed as Christ, for he himself will say: *I was a stranger and you welcomed me.* . . . All humility should be shown in addressing a guest upon arrival or departure. By a bow of the head or by a complete prostration of the body, Christ is to be adored because he is indeed welcomed in them. . . . Great care and concern are to be shown in receiving poor people and pilgrims because in them more particularly Christ is received. . . .[37]

Silence for Meditation

Questions to Ponder

- Think about a time when you were embarrassed about receiving a gift. What caused your embarrassment?
- How do you see others, especially when meeting those unknown to you?
- How can you practice seeing stranger (and friend) as Christ?

Psalm Fragment
Who is like the Lord our God,
who is seated on high... ?
He raises the poor from the dust,
and lifts the needy from the ash heap.
Psalm 113:5, 7

Journal Reflections

- What memories did the reflection stir in you?
- Have you ever welcomed another as Christ? What happened in you?
- When has welcoming others revealed the divine presence?

Prayer for Today
Today may I welcome each person as you, my Lord. Amen.

Knowing God's Hospitality
Day 34—Saturday

... extend hospitality to strangers.
Romans 12:13b

Your hospitality knows no bounds, Dearest Friend. You are the eternally gracious Host, welcoming me into broad and open spaces where my soul can breathe.

Dixie purchased an annual pass to the arboretum this year. She takes her camera and walks through woods and glades. Sometimes she takes our grandsons to the children's garden. They play largely unhindered by normal con-straints, running in fields and splashing in the water, soaking themselves.

It's an open place for all of us. I walk there with Dixie. Drawing in the sweet air of pine needles, I discover that pressing schedules and incessant obligations don't exist on forest paths.

My heart grows larger and more generous than normal, more humble and quiet. I feel my smallness amid the greatness of all you have made, Holy One.

It's an open space that opens space in the heart. I breathe and you are the air. I walk and return to the garden of beginnings, Eden. In silent communion, I discover you are the Host of a vast home where I am always welcome.

You made the world as a garden of freedom for our home, filling it with beauty and wonder, playfulness and joy. There is space for the heart to roam and wonder and praise.

Yes, we despoil your creation and abuse it. The garden of delight now holds threat, and we flinch at the snap of a twig in the bushes. Still, great and open spaces awaken awareness of your infinite grace and the immensity of your heart.

It was always your intention to enter and share the home you made for us. Sin didn't make you do it. Your love did. And when our brother Jesus appeared, he opened his arms to welcome all we are, all that we have been and will be.

"Abide in me," says Jesus. "For my heart is large and encompassing, gener-ous beyond imagination. Come and play as unhindered as children, free from all that wounds and constrains the soul's hunger to love. My heart is your home."

Biblical Wisdom

As the Father has loved me, so I have loved you; abide in my love . . . I have said these things to you so that my joy may be in you, and that your joy may be complete.
John 15: 9, 11

Theological Thoughts

The creator God has spread out for our delight a banquet that was twenty bil-lion years in the making. A banquet of rivers and lakes, of rain and sunshine, of rich earth and of amazing flowers, of handsome trees and dancing fishes, of contemplative animals and of whistling winds, of dry and wet seasons, of cold and hot climates . . . and so are we, blessings ourselves, invited to the banquet.[38]

Silence for Meditation

Questions to Ponder
- When do "open spaces" appear in your heart?
- How might creation be a spiritual practice for you?
- Where do you experience God's welcome so that you feel truly at home?

Psalm Fragment
They confronted me in the day of my calamity;
  but the Lord was my support.
He brought me out into a broad place;
  he delivered me, because he delighted in me.
  Psalm 18:18-19

Journal Reflections
- What experiences or awareness were stirred by today's reflection?
- When is creation a "spiritual banquet" for you?
- Slowly reflect on the final paragraph in today's reflection. What desires are moved in you?

Prayer for Today
Welcome me into your heart, O Lord, that my heart may be as big as yours. Amen.

Blessing the Enemy
Day 35—Monday

> *Bless those who persecute you; bless and do not curse them.*
> Romans 12:14

I wish it were my nature to bless, not curse, those who trouble me. It's your nature, my Brother, but I suspect blessing your enemies was not easy or pleasant for you either.

Pharisees and their friends argued with you as you went about preaching and healing. They condemned you for leading people away from the true way of God, for offending the glory of Lord. You were way too loose and took liberty with God's law and ancient tradition, interpreting it to suit yourself.

The powerful feared your followers would stir the Romans to unseat them from places of influence. They resisted you, denounced you, leveling blistering attacks for your words and the questionable people with whom you were comfortable—the unclean and common, the rejected and unacceptable.

And you argued with them. Is the Blessed Father a God of compassion or bondage? Does the Holy One set captives free and heal human souls or oppress them under the weight of ancient legalisms?

With sharp words, you denounced them as harshly as they condemned you. "Whitewashed tombs" and "hypocrites" you called them (Matthew 23:1-36). This doesn't sound like a blessing. I hear only anger and disgust.

But appearances hide other truth. You fought for a faithful knowledge of the Holy One, who surpasses all knowing. You struggled to reveal a God who does not divide the world into insiders and outsiders, who builds no walls to separate holy from unholy.

You battled to bring to light the God who obliterates the distinctions we make between ourselves and others—the distinctions we make so that we can admire the distance between ourselves and those we consider not as good or as right as we are.

You fought to reveal the God who is love, not regulation, the Blessed Mystery who eagerly welcomes all into the arms of immeasurable mercy.

Perhaps you were blessing them, Jesus. You wrestled with them to surrender arrogance and condemnation and come into the warm light of a grace which has neither beginning nor end. Then they, too, would become children of the Father, loving as God loves.

You blessed your enemies by inviting them to love freely.

Biblical Wisdom
But I say to you, Love your enemies and pray for those who persecute you, so that you may be children of your Father in heaven; for he makes his sun to rise on the evil and on the good. . . .
  Matthew 5:44-45

Theological Thoughts
That our wholeness as human beings depends upon living out the Great Commandment is the most fundamental of all early monastic convictions. The starting point in a life of prayer is to know, no matter how dimly, that we are created for and called to love. . . . Love is the final goal of a life of prayer, and loving and learning how to love are the daily work and pleasure in prayer.[39]

Silence for Meditation

Questions to Ponder
- Who or what is hardest for you to bless?
- How do you justify Jesus' fights with the command to bless?
- How have those who trouble you been an invitation to grow?

Psalm Fragment
May the Lord give strength to his people!
    May the Lord bless his people with peace!
  Psalm 29:11

Journal Reflections

- What helps us move through resentment toward blessing?
- Pray several days for a difficult person in your life. What changes do you notice in yourself?
- How are freedom, resentment, and blessing related?

Prayer for Today

Fill me with your love, that in freedom I may be your blessing. Amen.

Wisdom and Blessing
Day 36—Tuesday

> *Bless those who persecute you; bless and do not curse them.*
> Romans 12:14

You were a young man when your enemies killed you, Jesus. But you seem older, older than me, older than time, as if your heart should be dated not in years but from time immemorial, an old soul possessing incalculable wisdom.

"Father, forgive them," you said from the place of your torment. "Into your hands, I commend my spirit" (Luke 23:32-46).

These are the words of one who has surrendered everything to the Loving Mystery of God. It takes at least a lifetime to learn this, and most of us never do. We cling to the illusions that we can or should or need to control the conditions and outcomes of our lives.

Mothers surrender such illusion. They have felt the stir of new life in their wombs, a life with reasons and rhythms all its own. They know there is something far more crucial than self-interest—and that there comes a time to let go and simply trust.

The old, too, come to know this. With time and age, one arrives at a point where forces beyond self take over; there is nothing one can do to stop the changes that diminish and ultimately carry us off.

Such awareness de-centers the soul. We discover we are not the center of the universe. Life goes on beyond us, and the wise see that life must be spent on something larger and lasting, something that is the holy secret of life and joy—and of a beauty that outlasts us.

You knew this, Jesus. You knew the Loving Mystery from whom all life flows is unending generosity, continually pouring out the substance of divine life that we—that I—may know life and love.

And when we bless another, our souls participate in the life of God. We know God and share in the Love whom God is.

Some precious old souls who have blessed me intuitively knew this. They were like the prodigal's father, half-blind and worn out from worry, yet blessing and weeping at the lost one's return, little concerned with what had been lost.

It didn't matter. Only blessing mattered.

Biblical Wisdom
Jesus said, "Father forgive them; for they do not know what they are doing."
Luke 23:34

Theological Thoughts
Rembrandt [in his painting of the return of the Prodigal Son], who showed me the Father in utmost vulnerability, made me come to the awareness that my final vocation is indeed to become like the Father, and to live out his divine compassion in my daily life. . . . As the Father, I have to dare to carry the responsibility of an adult person and dare to trust that the real joy and real fulfillment can only come from welcoming home those who have been hurt . . . with a love that neither asks nor expects anything in return. . . . No power, no success, no popularity, no easy satisfaction.[40]

Silence for Meditation

Questions to Ponder
- In whom do you see Jesus' wisdom of surrendering all to God?
- What's the connection between wisdom and blessing others?
- To what are you giving your life? To what do you want to be given?

Psalm Fragment
You desire truth in the inward being;
> *therefore teach me wisdom in my secret heart.*
Psalm 51:6

Journal Reflections
- When have you recognized that "only blessing matters"?
- What experiences help you "to let go and simply trust?"
- What are your challenges as you become like the Father (see Theological Thoughts)?

Prayer for Today
Make me a wise, old soul like you, Jesus, knowing that only blessing matters. Amen.

Journey Week Seven

Rejoice with those who rejoice, weep with those who weep.
Romans 12:15

Sharing Joy
Day 37

Communing with the Saints
Day 38—Holy Thursday

Becoming the Christ
Day 39—Good Friday

Sacramental Life
Day 40

Sharing Joy
Day 37—Wednesday

Rejoice with those who rejoice....
Romans 12:15

The phone rings. Scott speaks. I hold my breath.

Will he be one more case of cancer in a year filled with health threats?

I know the news before he finishes the sentence. No heaviness burdens his tone. No cancer. No great threat. Relief.

Laughter dances off the office walls as he shares the story and looks to the day he can return to work, and play without restraint with his young children. A joy shared is a joy magnified, and Scott multiplies his joy with every phone call.

And I am blessed to share it. I hang up the receiver lighter, more human and alive than when I picked it up.

An old icon hangs on my office wall, the great overseer of all that happens there. It reveals the truth of this shared moment . . . and of all time.

The icon shows three figures sitting at a small, square table. Each leans slightly toward the other. An exquisite intimacy radiates among them as each silently shares the secret substance of his being with the others, while receiving their substance into himself.

The substance is love. For the figures reveal your Triune nature, Loving Mystery. As the Father, you are the Infinite Source of Love, pouring yourself out in the Son, who is Love's speaking and acting; and in the Holy Spirit, you are the unending, inexhaustible activity of Love in the world.

There is an empty place in the icon. The fourth side of the table is unoccupied. And you invite me to pull up a chair and sit down. I belong there, in the circle of your loving, intimately receiving and sharing your substance.

This is my place, now and for eternity. And you constantly draw me and all that is to the table, into the circle of your inexhaustible love.

Scott calls, and without a thought we are swept into the great giving and receiving of your life, as joy and care pass between us.

We took our place at the table, and the faces in the icon smiled.

Biblical Wisdom
Beloved, let us love one another, because love is from God; everyone who loves is born of God and knows God.
    1 John 4:7

Theological Thoughts

To be comforted does not mean that we receive something, a thing, an object from God but that we catch sight of the beauty and splendor of God. Where, then, do we see that? Where can we find that? . . . The beauty, the splendor of God is visible in all who prepare God's way.[41]

Silence for Meditation

Questions to Ponder
· When do you become "more human and alive" in sharing with others?
· When do you experience "your place," feeling at home in God's love?
· What does the "circle of love" in the icon tell you about the Trinity?

Psalm Fragment
You show me the path of life.
        In your presence there is fullness of joy;
        in your right hand are pleasures forevermore.
    Psalm 16:11

Journal Reflections
· Imagine yourself at the table in the icon. What is it like? What do you receive?
· What experiences are stirred by the reflection?
· What relationships invite you into "fuller participation in the one and mutual Love"?

Prayer for Today
Bring me to the table of your life, that I may receive and give as you. Amen.

Communing with the Saints
Day 38—Holy Thursday

Rejoice with those who rejoice, weep with those who weep.
   Romans 12:15

It's a silent space that whispers a grace walls cannot contain. I happened upon it just inside an old church in San Antonio.

Stepping in the door, I turned left and found myself in a tiny prayer chapel, lit by candles and what light flows through a west window high above. A hundred faces or more gazed at me in the darkness, looking at me from photos pinned to the wall above a rack of candles.

Some faces were weary and worn, near the end of their days; others smiled, aglow with the sweet bloom of youth. Young men and women stood erect in military uniforms. Children smiled from the safety of back yards. Middle-aged faces, too, looked out at me, smiles dimmed by the wear of mid-life malaise.

Each face bore a secret need. And some soul who loves them came here and pinned their fondest hopes and deepest fears to the wall . . . and lit a candle, each flickering wick a silent cry for mercy.

And you whispered from every face, Holy One: "Bring it all. Bring all you are, all that's in your heart, all you fear, all for which you hope. Hold nothing back."

And I prayed, first standing, then on my knees, welcomed by the faces, pleading for every need that hung on the wall. You joined me with each one in a communion of hope and hunger for the Love that heals every wound. For you, my Lord.

I rejoiced with those who rejoiced and wept with those who mourned. And even the weeping was joy, for I was joined in one holy communion of saints with every soul whose face gazed at me.

And I was a human being, as human as you my Brother, who welcomes all that is human into yourself, embracing it with the Love for which no name is enough. We were one, joined in one body of beseeching for final redemption.

In shared joy and sorrow, your kingdom was as real as my tears.

Biblical Wisdom
He is the image of the invisible God, the firstborn of all creation; for in him
all things . . . were created, things visible and invisible, . . . all things have
been created through him and for him.
    Colossians 1:15-16

Theological Thoughts

To understand the incarnation as occasioned by human sin and having the primary purpose of atoning for that sin—the perspective of Anselm of Canterbury and the "Satisfaction Theory"—would suggest that the primary purpose of ministry is the overcoming and elimination of sin. To understand the incarnation as bringing creation to completion—the perspective of Franciscan tradition—would suggest . . . that ministry is primarily about fostering genuine humanness in the pattern of Jesus Christ.[42]

Silence for Meditation

Questions to Ponder
- Where do you experience true communion with the saints?
- When have you been moved to be as human as Jesus?
- How does praying with and for others join you with them?

Psalm Fragment
I will give thanks to the LORD with my whole heart,
        in the company of the upright, in the congregation.
    Psalm 111:1

Journal Reflections
- What experiences does the reflection stir?
- How does deep communion with others change you?
- Jesus does not satisfy God's justice and pay a debt but comes to join all things to himself (Theological Thoughts). How does this affect the way you see his cross and ministry?

Prayer for Today

Draw all that we are into you, that we may share in one holy communion. Amen.

Becoming the Christ
Day 39—Good Friday

Rejoice with those who rejoice, weep with those who weep.
Romans 12:15

Hana kissed me up one side of my face and then the other. She kissed my forehead and chin, my nose, and each eye lid. Hana was five, and I was carrying her, pushing through a crowded little house on the outskirts of Addis Ababa, Ethiopia.

She wanted my attention as she sat on my left arm. When kissing me wasn't enough to get it, she took my face in her little brown hands, one hand on either side, so that we were nose to nose, eye to eye.

"Look at me," she seemed to say, without speaking. "Look at me. Let me know I am important to you. Show me that I am a human being, that I deserve your care, your attention."

But it wasn't Hana who cried out in needy silence. It was you, my Lord. You cried from the depth of her heart, hungry to be loved by the likes of me.

And it wasn't me who shifted her weight into both my arms and hugged the life and joy back into her. It was you, hungry in me, too, to love this little child, so cast off and unwanted by her fearful community.

They were afraid of the disease that killed her father and would soon kill her mother, leaving Hana and her brother orphans, AIDS orphans like so many others in this place.

They didn't know that you, dearest Friend, dwelt deeply in her. They could not fathom that in knowing her they would know you. In welcoming her, they would welcome you. In enfolding her in gentle arms, they would become the love you are.

In sharing joy and sorrow, fullness and need, they would become your flesh and blood. Like us.

Enfolded in each other's arms in a crowded house, on a sultry East African afternoon, Hana and I looked more like you on your cross than, perhaps, we ever will.

Open your arms, my Crucified Friend, and hold us in your embrace.

Biblical Wisdom
I am completing what is lacking in Christ's afflictions for the sake of his body, that is, the church. . . . To them God chose to make known how great among the Gentiles are the riches of the glory of this mystery, which is Christ in you. . . .
Colossians 1:24, 27

Theological Thoughts
In the Incarnation, God enters a glorious exchange with humanity, an exchange . . . in which God is Giver, Given and Gift/ing. The Gift and Giving is God's presence to the human reality, in its joys and delights as well as in its woundedness and fragility. . . . Human life and destiny are ultimately realized not in the exercise of individual rights and liberties, but in all those creative expressions of Love that lead to fuller communion in the one Love.[43]

Silence for Meditation

Questions to Ponder
- When are you aware of Christ in you, moving you?
- Do you ever hear Christ crying out in others' needs?
- Have you experienced Christ's flesh and blood through an act of caring?

Psalm Fragment
But I am a worm, and not human;
scorned by others, and despised by the people.
Psalm 22:6

Journal Reflections

- What memories are stirred by today's reflection?
- Where does Christ call you to complete his suffering in solidarity with others?
- When have you experienced "fuller communion with others in the one Love"?

Prayer for Today

Embrace all that we are and free us to share in your suffering love. Amen.

Sacramental Life
Day 40—Saturday

Rejoice with those who rejoice, weep with those who weep.
Romans 12:15

You shared it all, Jesus. Nothing is left out. Now at the end, your arms spread wide, you gasp a final breath: "It is finished" (John 19:30).

You took the fullness of what we are into yourself. You knew friendship and fought enemies. You loved and were let down by those you most loved . . . and needed. You drank wine and broke bread amid laughter at hospitable tables, and you tasted your own blood, hated and alone.

On your final days, tender hands washed your feet and anointed you with oil for unimaginable sorrow. You sparred again with opponents and knew the joy of washing, touching, blessing the feet of friends. You prayed for deliverance and delivered yourself into the hands of the Loving Mystery.

You were a stranger to nothing that is human, to nothing that is in me. You embraced all that we try to escape because it is too frightening, too messy, too painful.

And in your dying, you proclaimed it all finished. All that was and is human—pain and joy, sorrow, death, and the sweet delight of loving and being loved—all of it was taken into your heart.

The suffering of every human soul had become your suffering. Our weakness and mortality had become yours.

Refusing to be a master over us, you became our Brother, *my Brother,* sharing all that I am. All of it is taken into you and joined with the fullness of all you share in intimate communion with the Loving Mystery you call Father.

Every moment—my living and dying, my successes and failures, my joy and shame, my strength and fear—all of it now becomes one more sacramental moment in which the Love you are is shared with me and becomes part of me.

The world is lit up from within by your loving presence. So I can embrace it all, just as you did. I can weep with those who weep and mourn with those who mourn. I can welcome it all with sweetest joy, fearing no death because the end is always life and love, filling even me.

What more could I want?

Biblical Wisdom
I pray that you may have the power to comprehend . . . what is the breadth and length and height and depth, and to know the love of Christ that surpasses knowledge, so that you may be filled with the fullness of God.
Ephesians 3:18-19

Theological Thoughts
God the blessed Trinity . . . as he is eternal . . . just so was it in his eternal purpose to create human nature, which fair nature was first prepared for his own Son . . . . . [He] joined and united us to himself, and . . . in the joining he is our very true spouse and we his beloved wife . . . with which . . . he was never displeased, for he says: I love you and you love me, and our love will never part.[44]

Silence for Meditation

Questions to Ponder
- How do you experience Jesus as "your Brother"?
- When do you experience union with Jesus?
- How does union with Jesus free you to "welcome it all"?

Psalm Fragment
Return, O my soul, to your rest,
> *for the* Lord *has dealt bountifully with you.*
Psalm 116:7-8

Journal Reflections
- What does the description of Jesus' last days move in you?
- Jesus takes in all we are and shares all he is. What do you want to release to him?
- What do you want from Jesus?

Prayer for Today
May we constantly abide in union with you, who are endless love and eternal delight. Amen.

Notes

1   Martin Luther, in Tuomo Mannermaa, *Christ Present in Faith: Luther's View of Justification* (Minneapolis: Fortress Press, 2005), 21-22.

2   Luke Timothy Johnson, *The Writings of the New Testament: An Interpretation* (Minneapolis: Fortress Press, 1999), 345, 361-363; Brendan Byrne, S.J., *Romans* (Collegeville: Liturgical, 1996), 361-381.

3   Martin Luther, "A Simple Way to Pray," in *Luther's Works, Vol. 43, Devotional Writings II*, ed. Gustav K. Wiencke (Philadelphia: Fortress Press, 1968), 187-211.

4   Martin Luther, "A Brief Instruction in What to Look for and Expect in the Gospels," in *Luther's Works, Vol. 35, Word and Sacrament I*, ed. E. Theodore Bachmann (Philadelphia: Fortress Press, 1960), 121.

5   William A. Barry & William J. Connolly, *The Practice of Spiritual Direction* (San Francisco: HarperSanFrancisco, 1982), 17.

6   David L. Miller, "Where Beauty Lives," in *The Lutheran*, September 2004, 58.

7   Thomas Merton, *New Seeds of Contemplation* (New York: New Directions, 1961), 10.

8   Robert Barron, *And Now I See . . . A Theology of Transformation* (New York: Crossroad, 1998), 4.

9   Luther in Mannermaa, 21-22.

10 Merton, 21.

11   Joseph of Panephysis, in *The Doubleday Christian Quotation Collection*, compiled by Hannah Ward and Jennifer Wild (New York: Doubleday, 1997), 22.

12   Michael Downey, *Altogether Gift: A Trinitarian Spirituality* (Maryknoll: Orbis, 2000), 77.

13   Michael W. Blastic, "Attentive Compassion: Franciscan Resources for Ministry," in *Handbook of Spirituality for Ministers: Perspectives for the 21st Century, Volume 2* (Mahwah: Paulist, 2000), 252.

14   Margaret Silf, *Inner Compass: An Invitation to Ignatian Spirituality* (Chicago: Loyola Press, 1999), 183.

15   Julian of Norwich, *Showings*, The Classics of Western Spirituality (Mahwah: Paulist, 1978), 168.

16   Roberta C. Bondi, *To Love as God Loves: Conversations with the Early Church* (Philadelphia: Fortress Press, 1987), 30, 33-34.

17   Jürgen Moltmann, *The Source of Life: The Holy Spirit and the Theology of Life* (Minneapolis: Fortress Press, 1997), 19-20.

18   William A. Barry, *Finding God in All Things* (Notre Dame: Ave Maria Press, 1991), 38.

19   Merton, 15-16.

20   Downey, 38, 45.

21   Henri J.M. Nouwen, *Life of the Beloved* (New York: Crossroad, 1992), 98-99.

22   Saint Augustine, *Confessions*, translated by Henry Chadwick (Oxford: Oxford University Press, 1991), 201.

23   Henri J.M. Nouwen, *Making All Things New* (San Francisco: HarperSanFrancisco, 1981), 23-24, 37.

24   Moltmann, 10-11, 84.

25   Merton, 1, 3.

26 Jean-Pierre De Caussade, *The Sacrament of the Present Moment*, translated by Kitty Muggeridge (San Francisco: HarperSanFrancisco, 1981), 1, 3.

27 Carlo Carretto, *The God Who Comes*, quoted in *A Guide to Prayer for Ministers & Other Servants*, (Nashville: The Upper Room, 1991), 15.

28 Julian, 152, 225.

29 Dermot A. Lane, "Death, the Self, Memory, and Hope," in *Handbook of Spirituality for Ministers: Perspectives for the 21st Century, Volume 2* (Mahwah: Paulist, 2000), 100.

30 Ronald Rolheiser, *The Holy Longing* (New York: Doubleday, 1999), 147.

31 Abba Allois in *Western Asceticism*, The Library of Christian Classics, ed. Owen Chadwick (Philadelphia: Westminster, 1958), 132.

32 William H. Shannon, *Silence on Fire: Prayer of Awareness* (New York: Crossroad, 1991), 20.

33 Elizabeth A. Dreyer, *Passionate Spirituality: Hildegard of Bingen and Hadewijch of Brabant* (Mahwah: Paulist, 2005), 146.

34 Merton, 67.

35 *Western Asceticism*, 184-185.

36 Silf, 127.

37 St. Benedict, *The Rule of Saint Benedict*, ed. Timothy Fry (New York: Vintage, 1998), 51-52.

38 Matthew Fox, *Original Blessing* (New York: Jeremy P. Tarcher/Putnam, 2000), 112-113.

39 Roberta C. Bondi, *To Pray & To Love: Conversations on Prayer with the Early Church* (Minneapolis: Fortress Press, 1991), 28.

40 Henri J.M. Nouwen, *The Return of the Prodigal Son* (New York: Doubleday, 1992), 121, 132.

41   Dorothee Soelle, *Theology for Skeptics* (Minneapolis: Fortress Press, 1995), 126.

42   Blastic, 258.

43   Downey, 81, 86.

44   Julian, 293.